This Book Belongs To:

_____

- - - - - - - - - - - - - - - - - - - -

_____

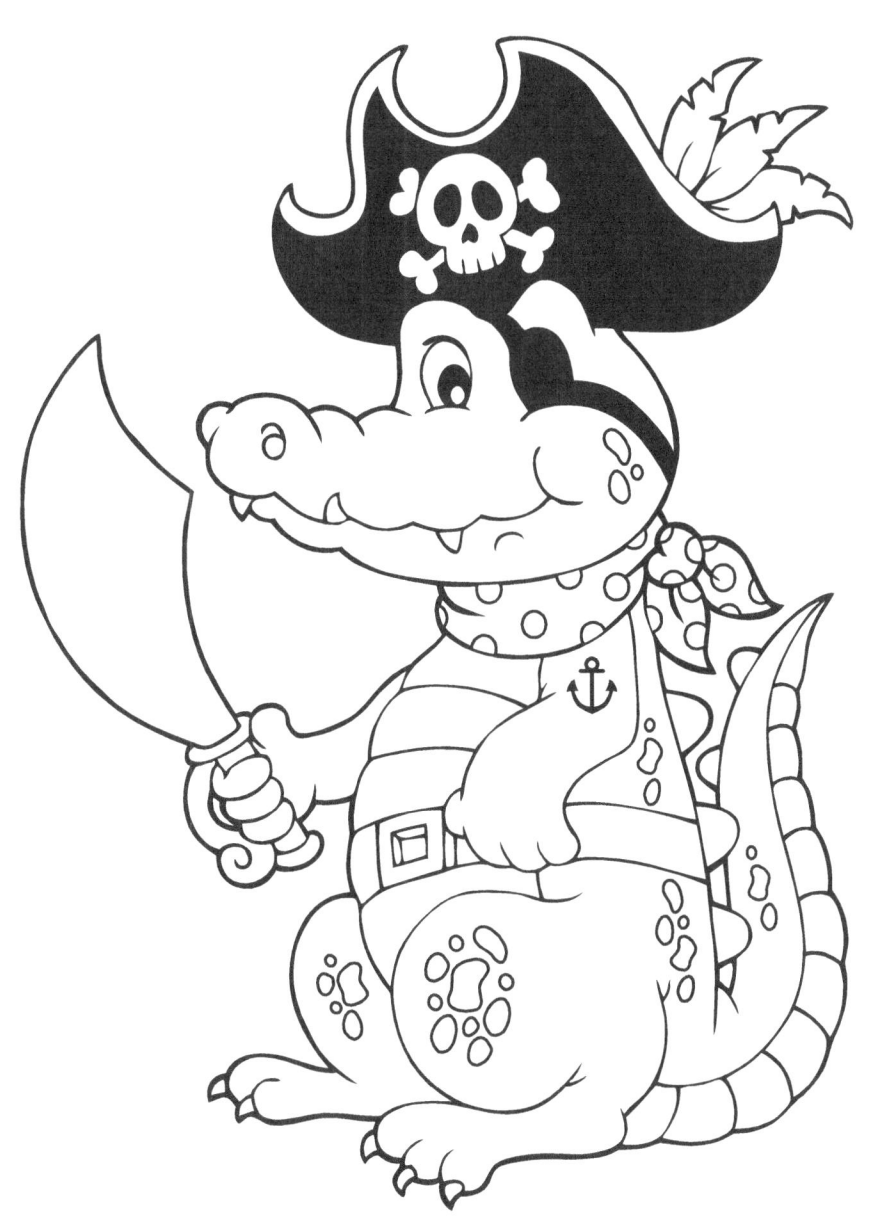

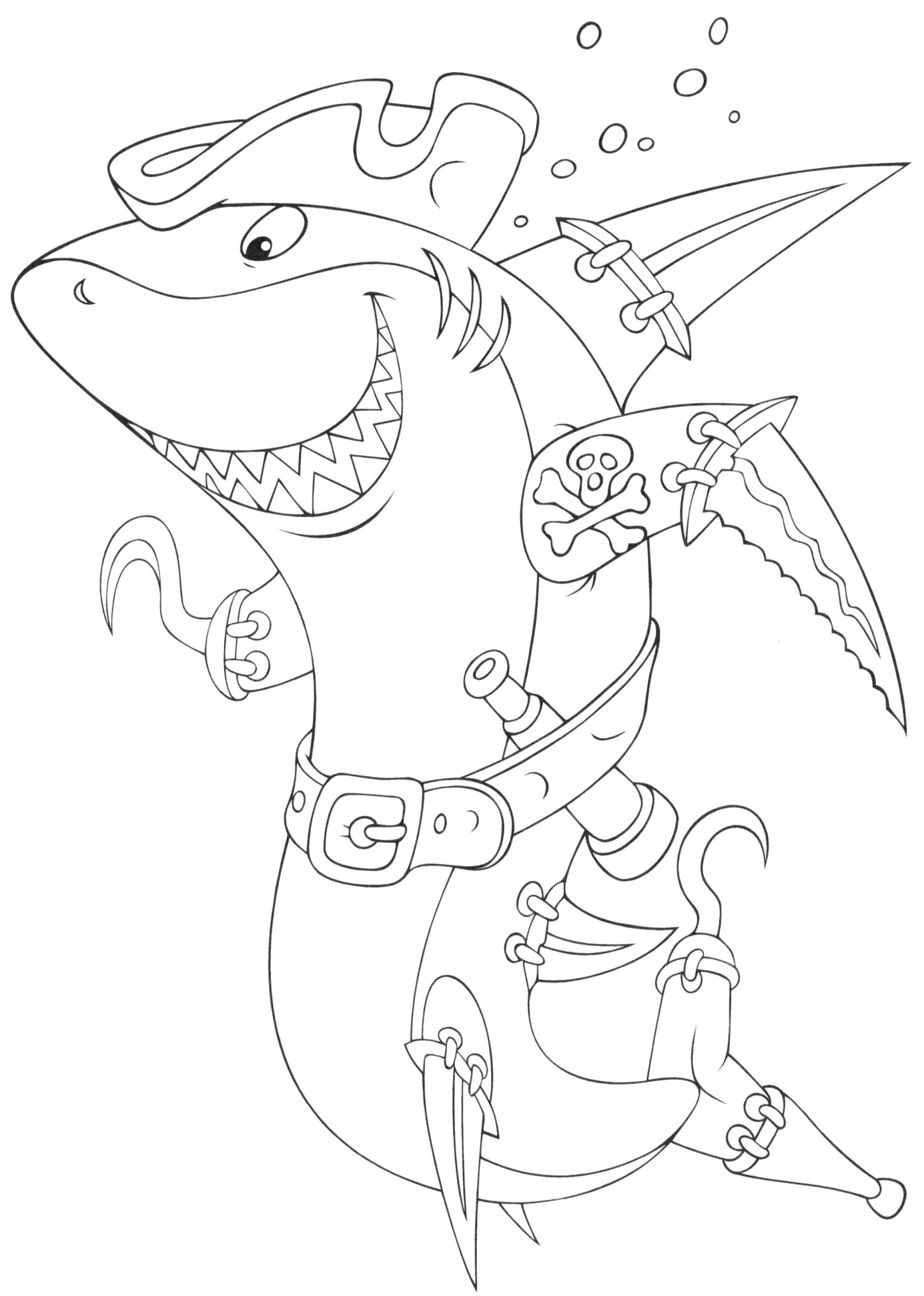

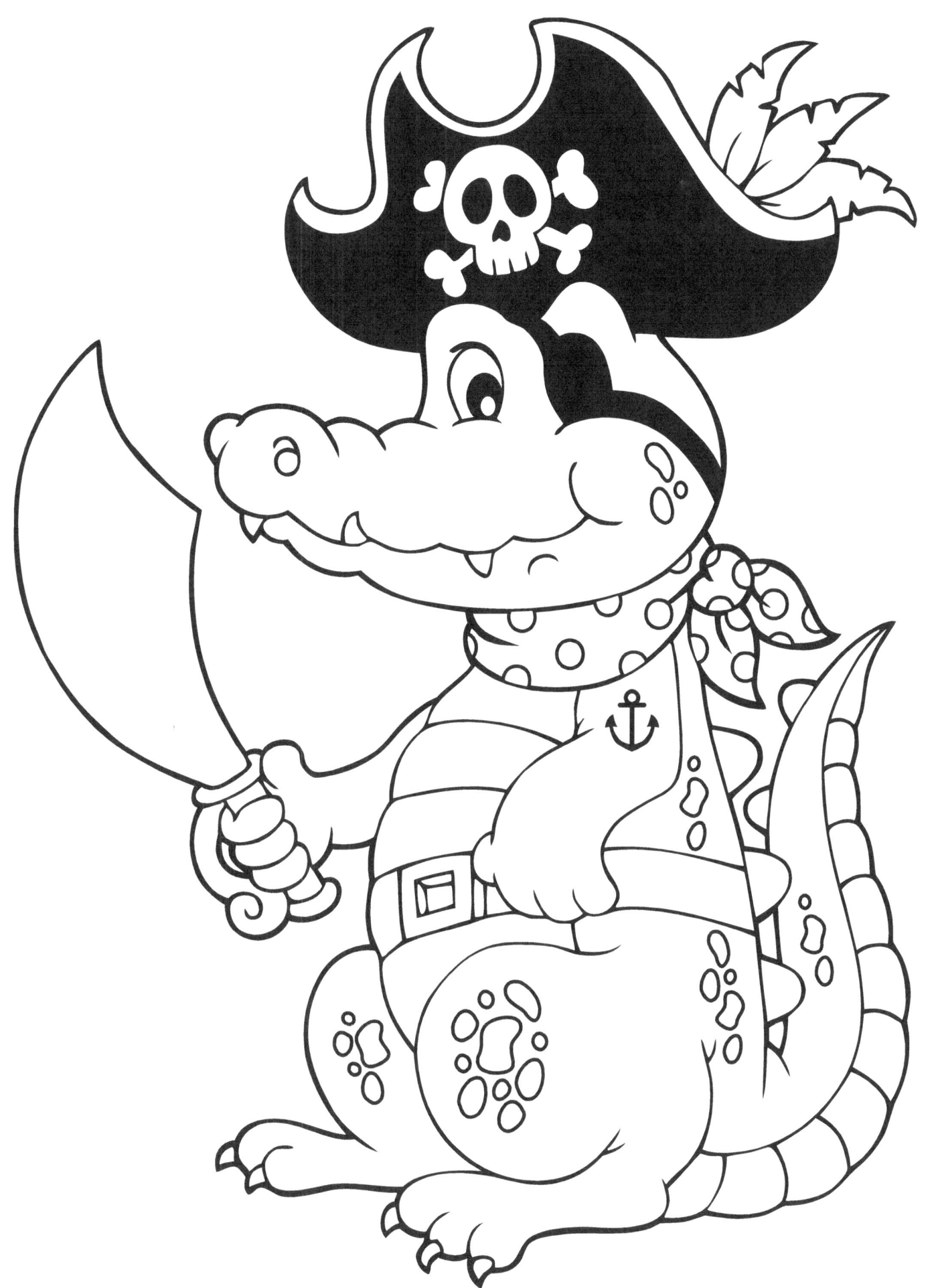

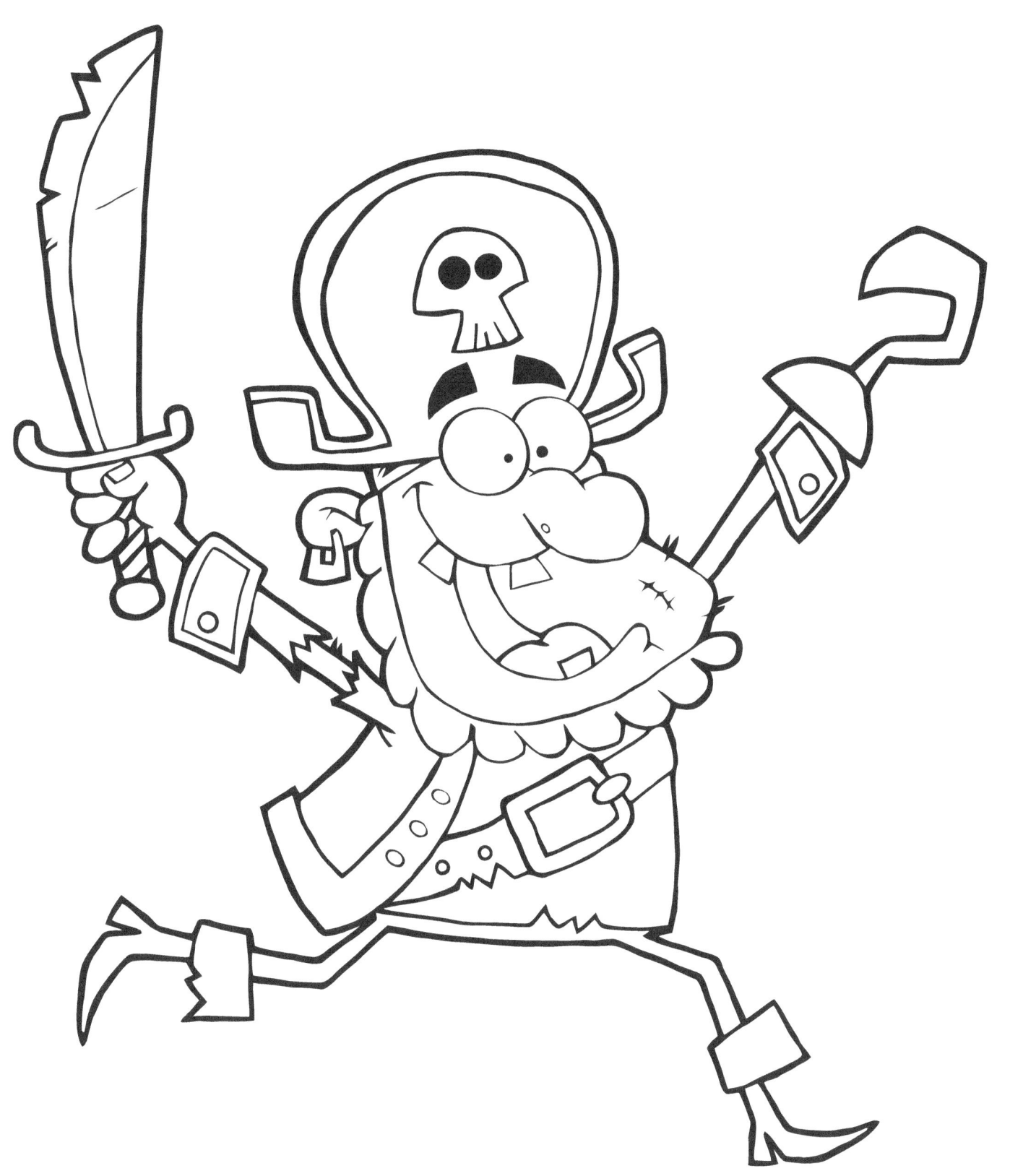

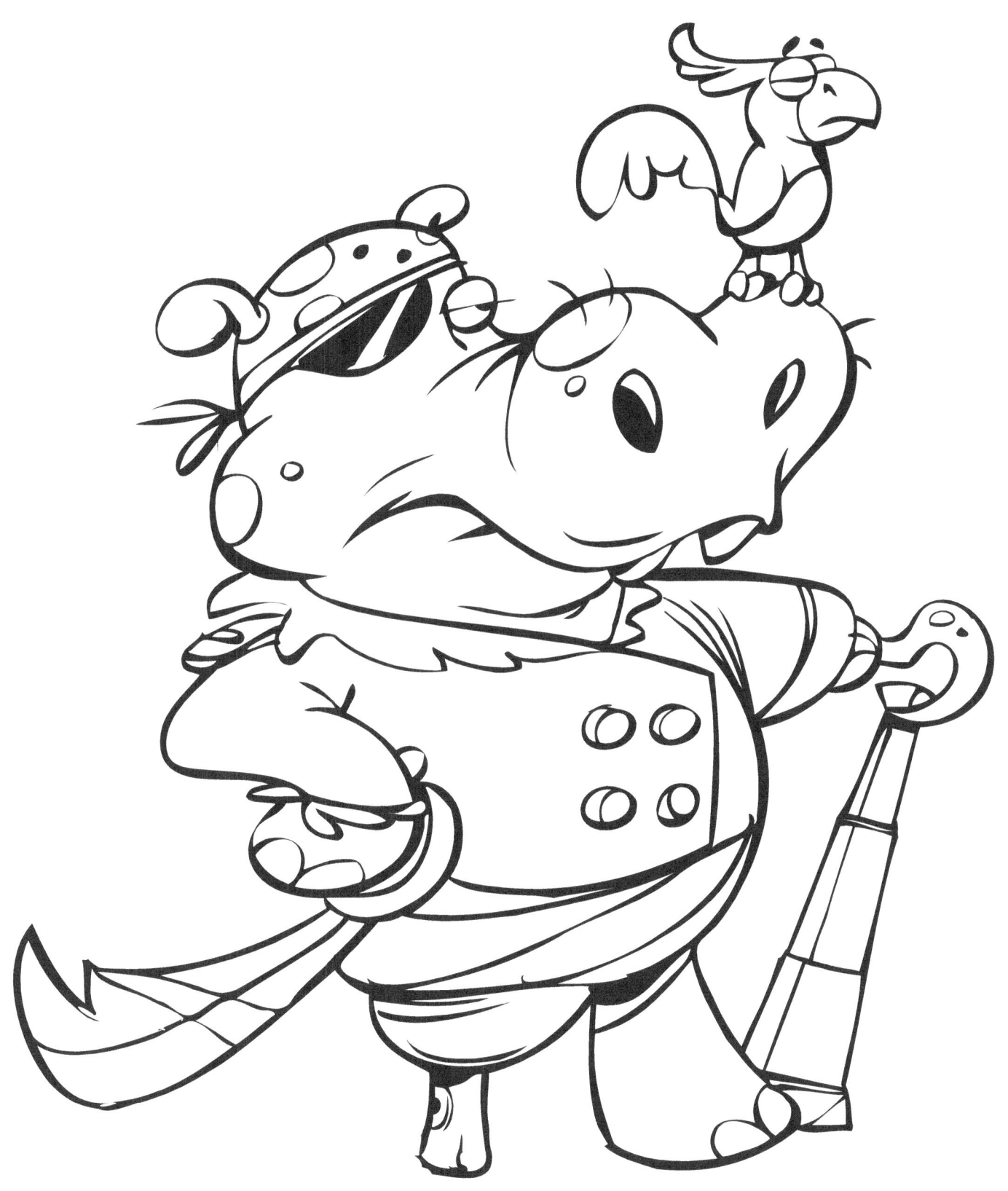

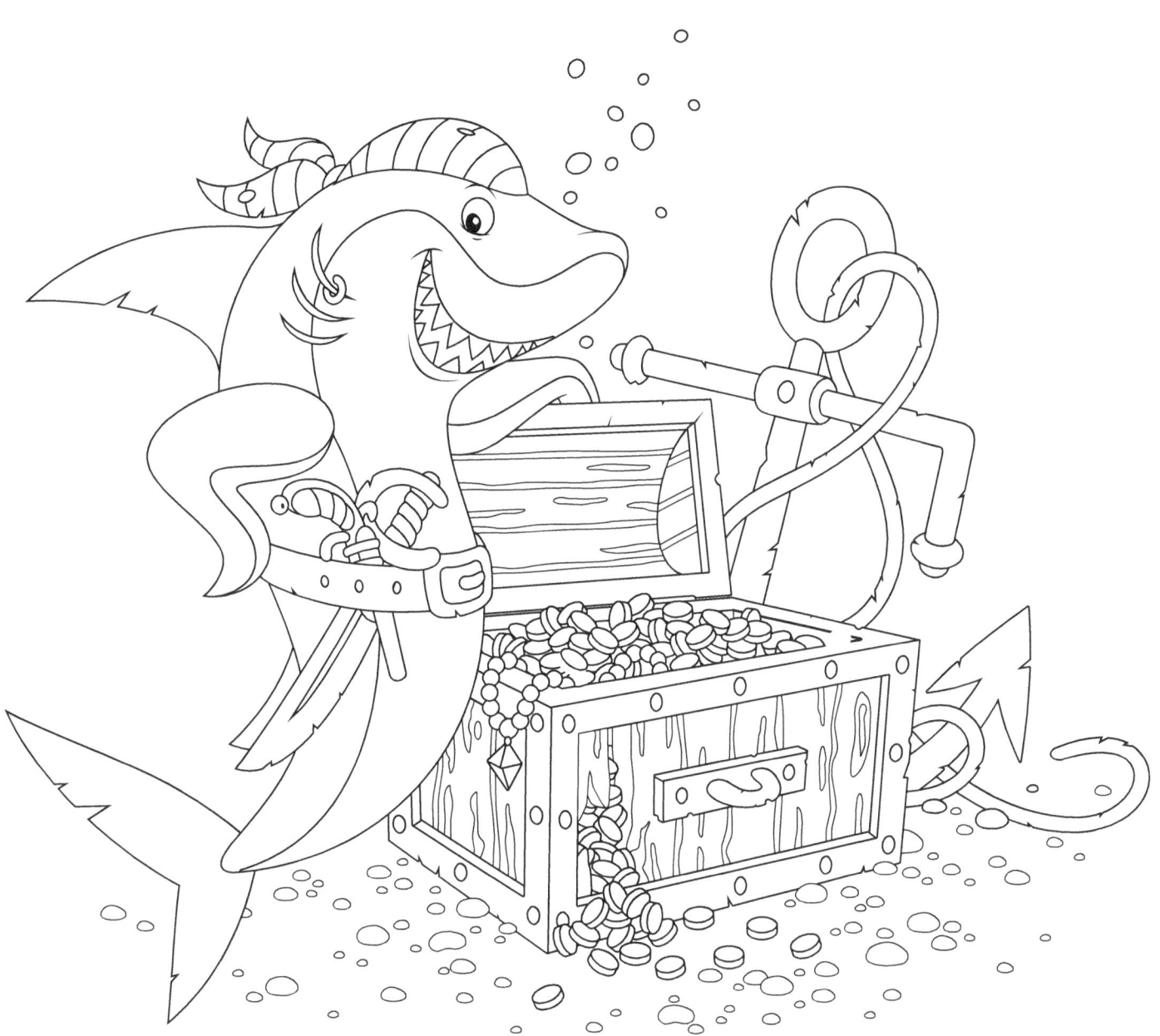

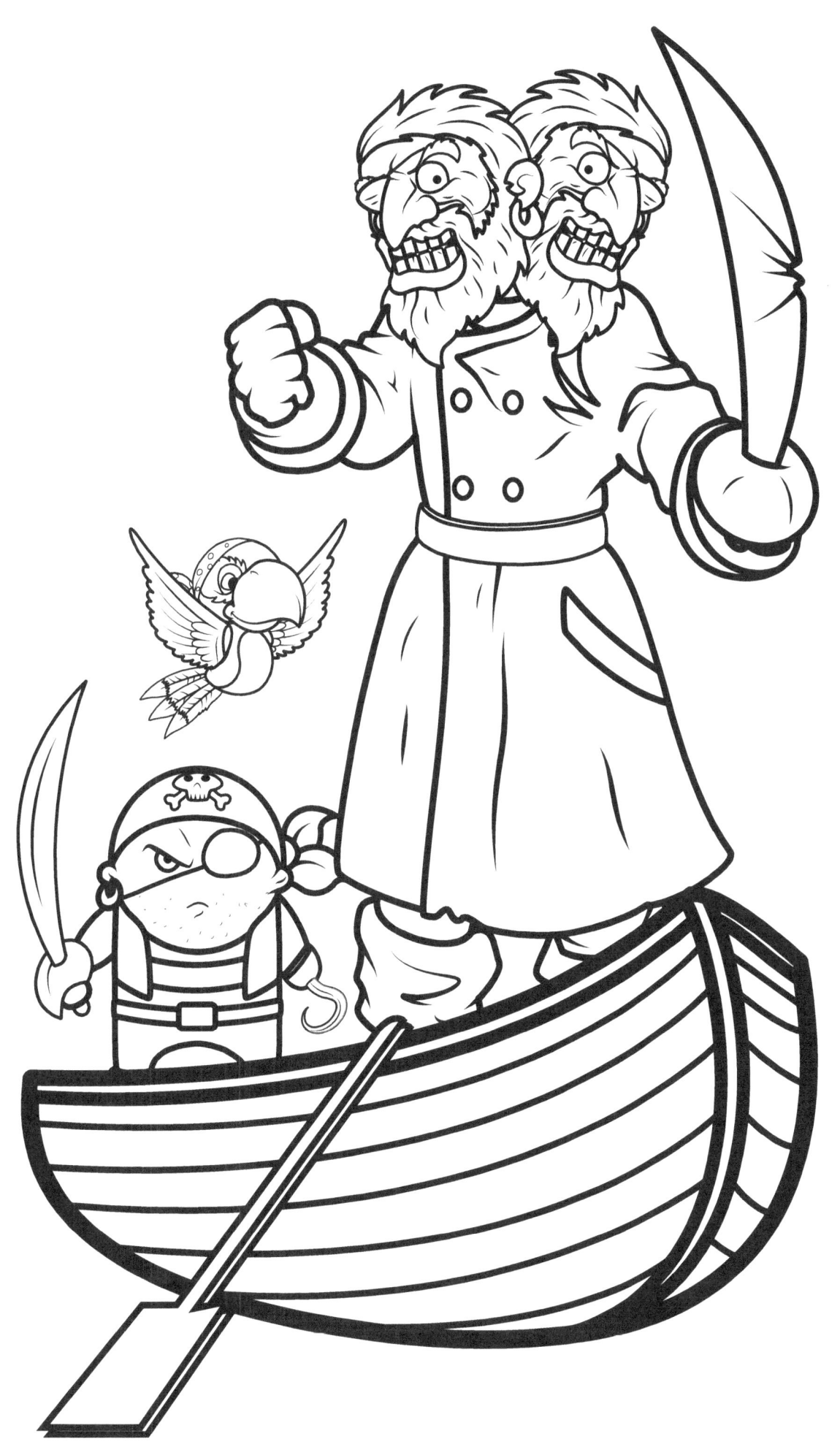

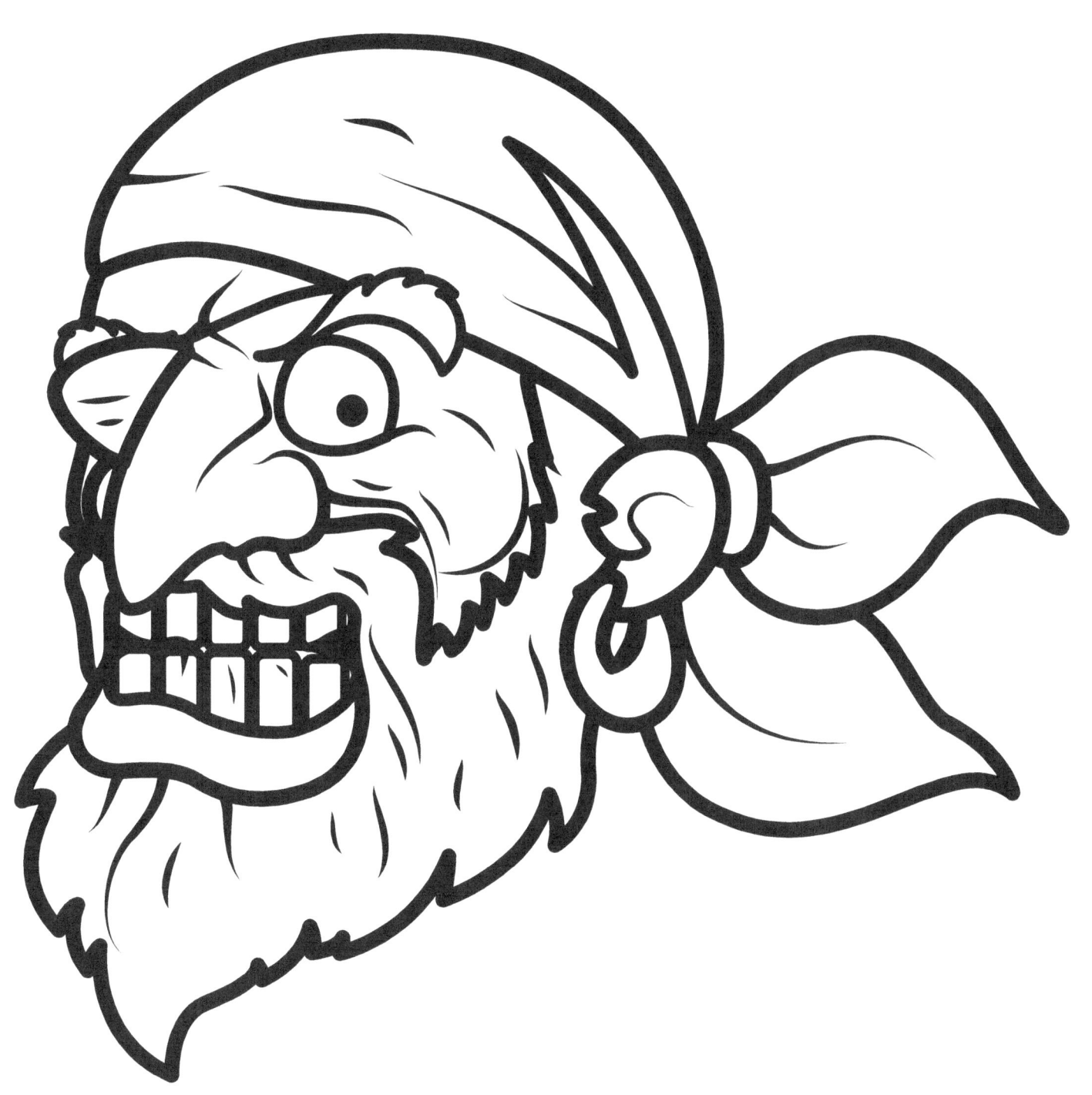

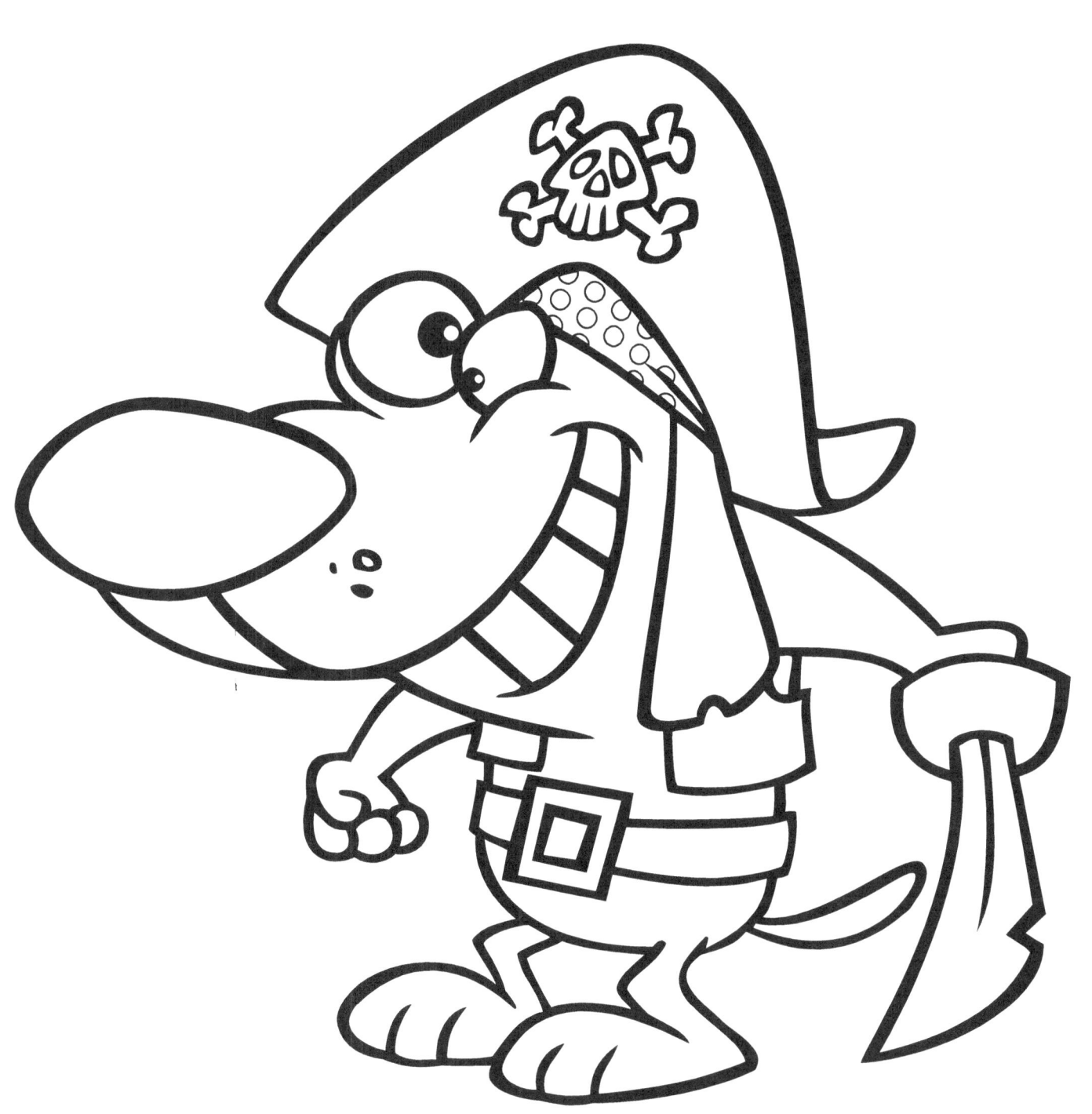

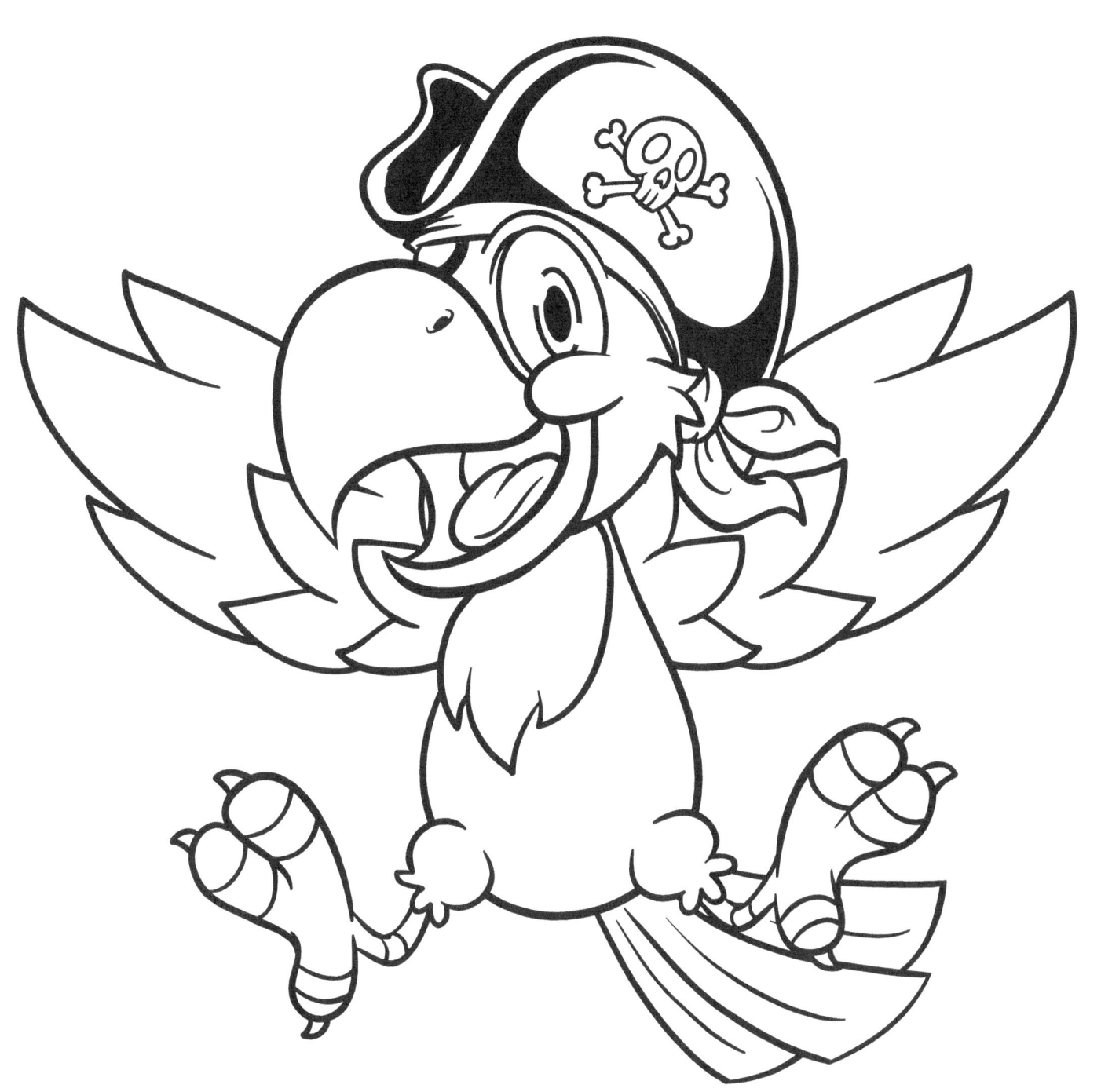

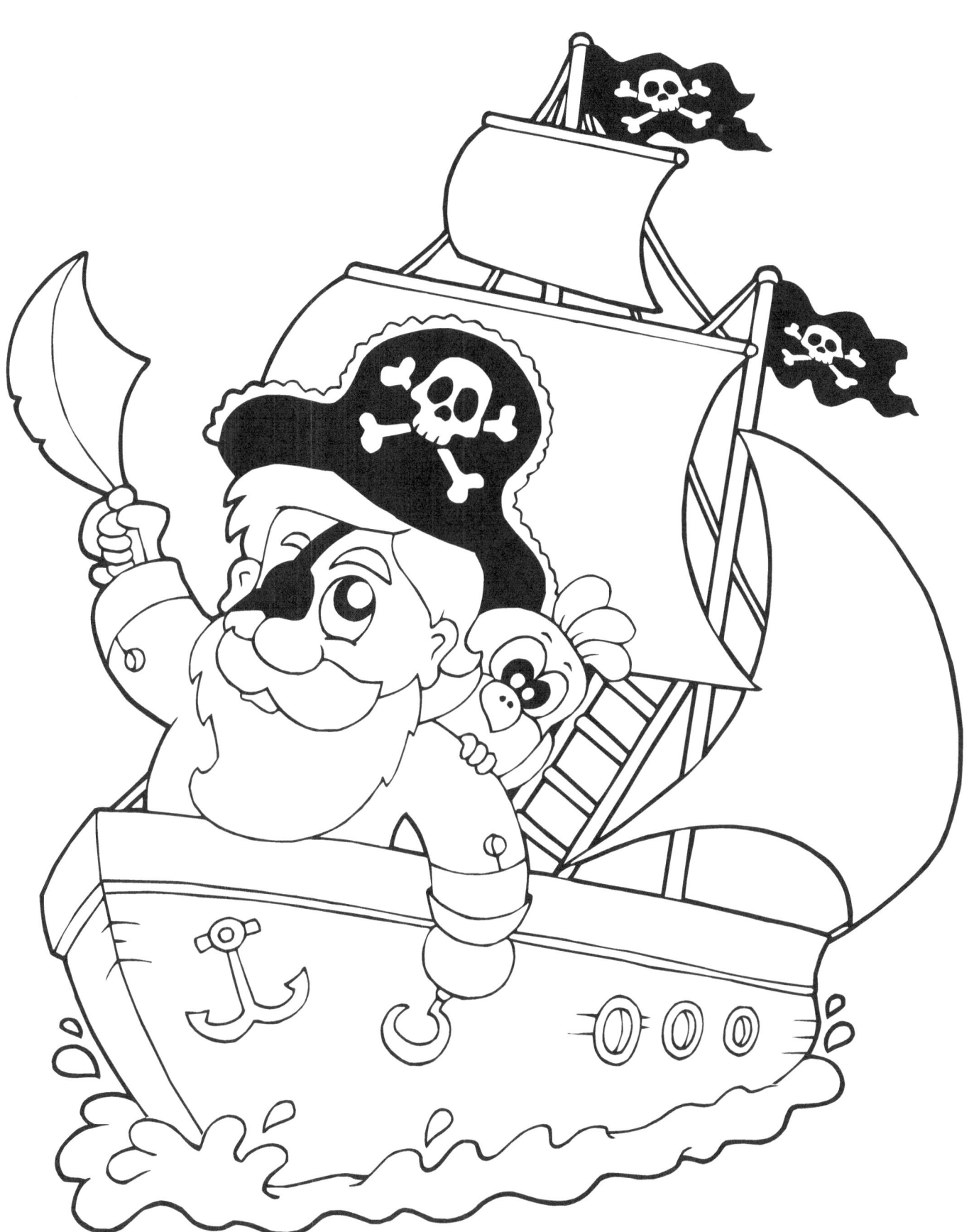

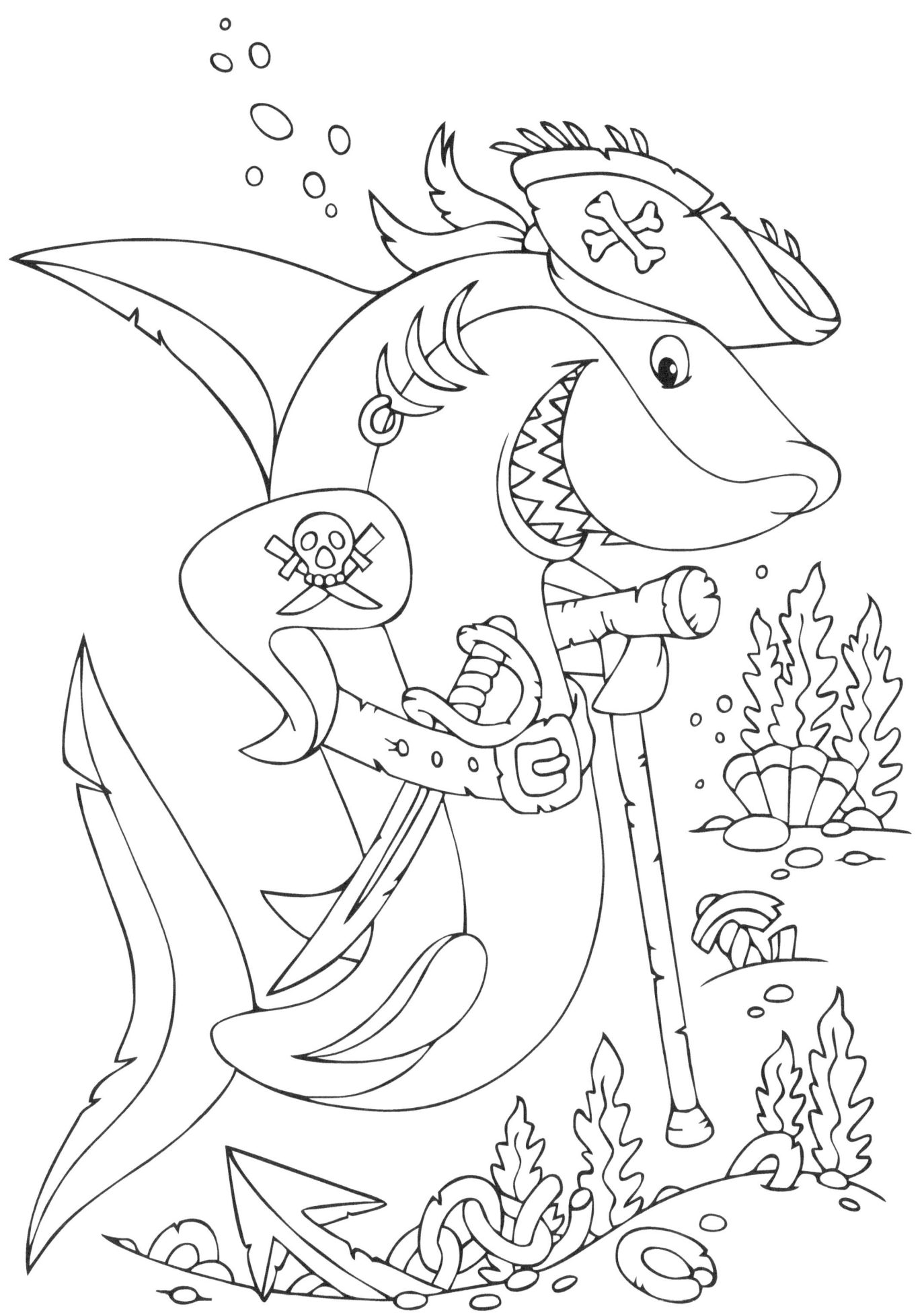

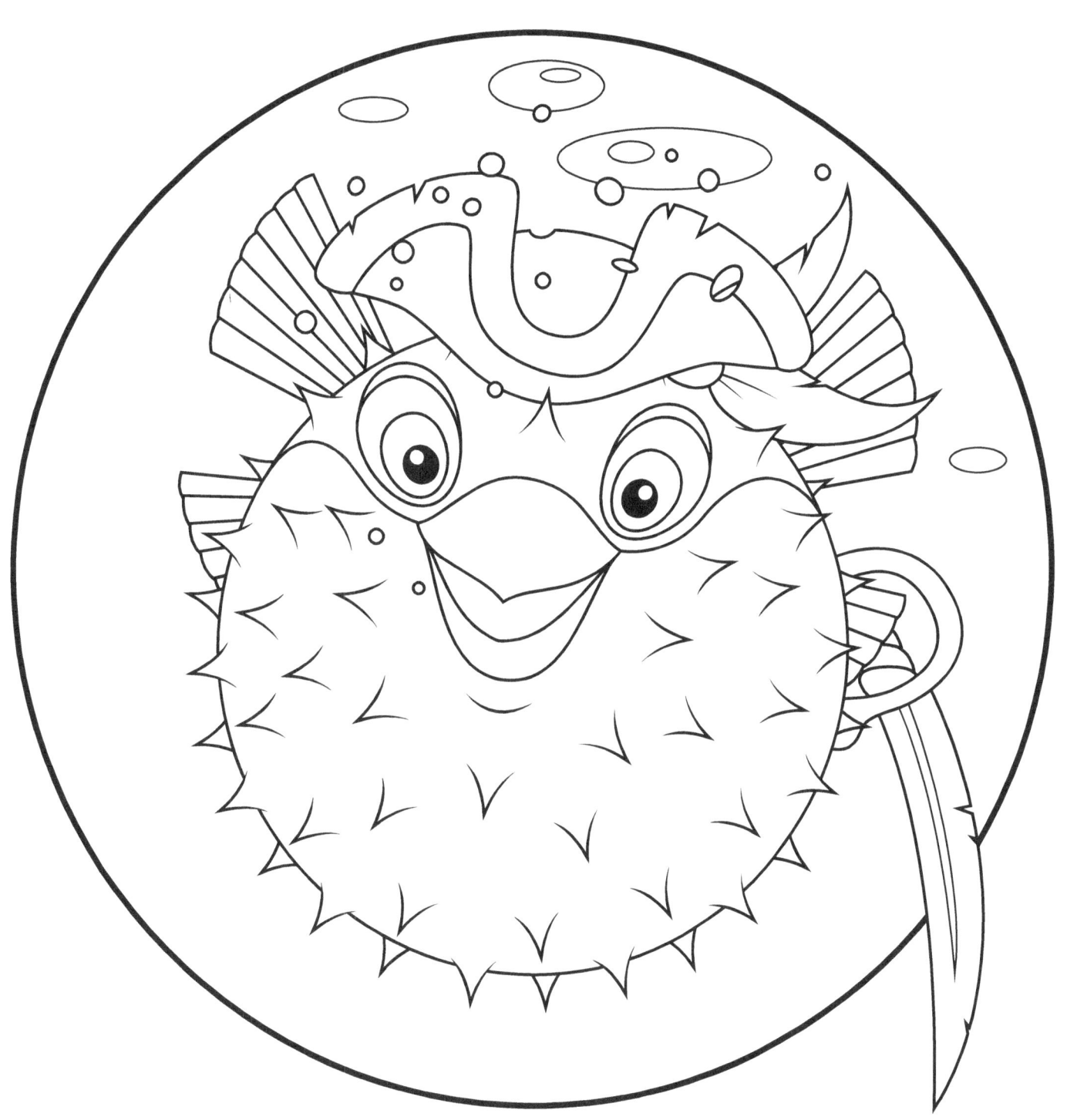

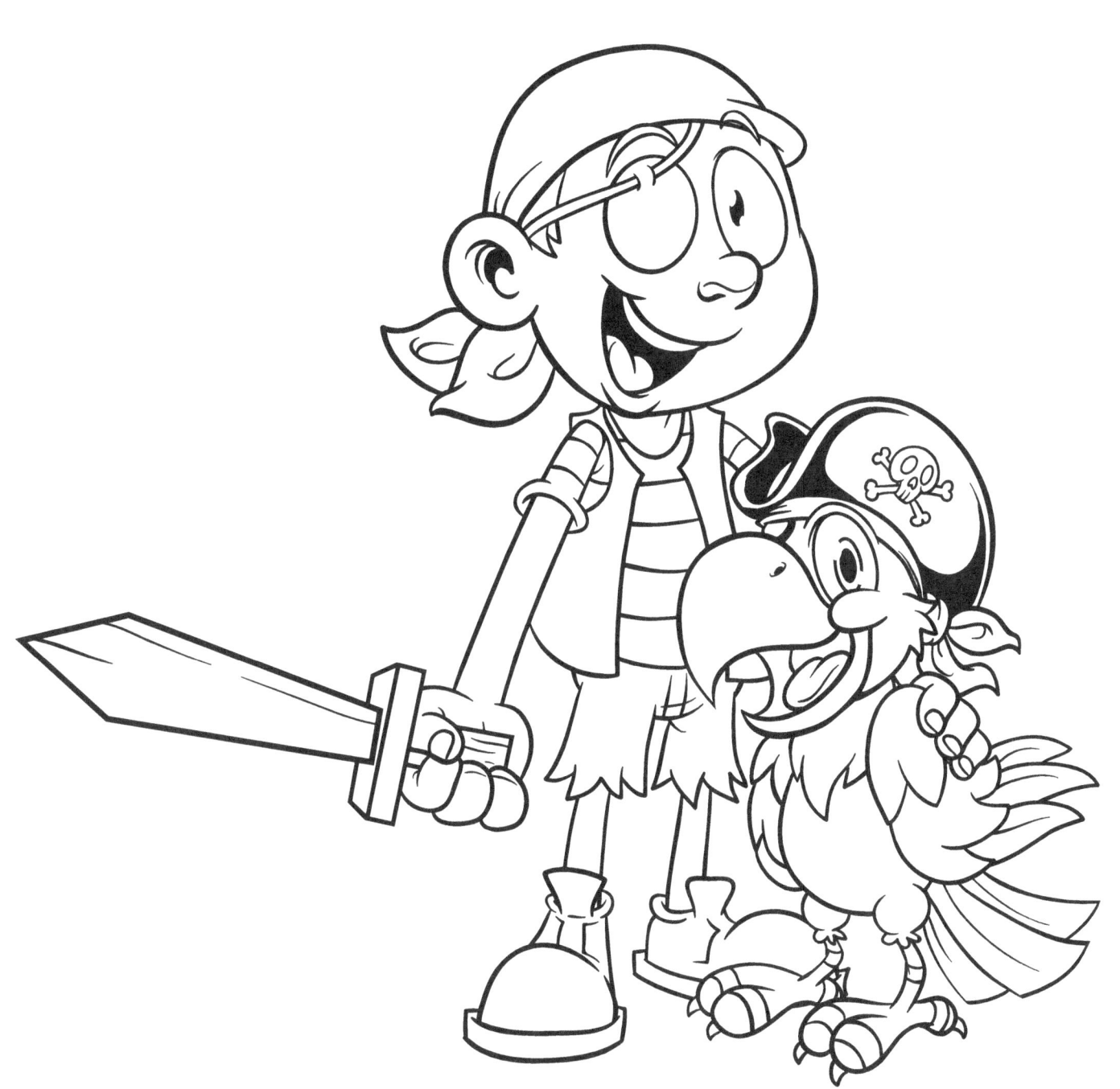

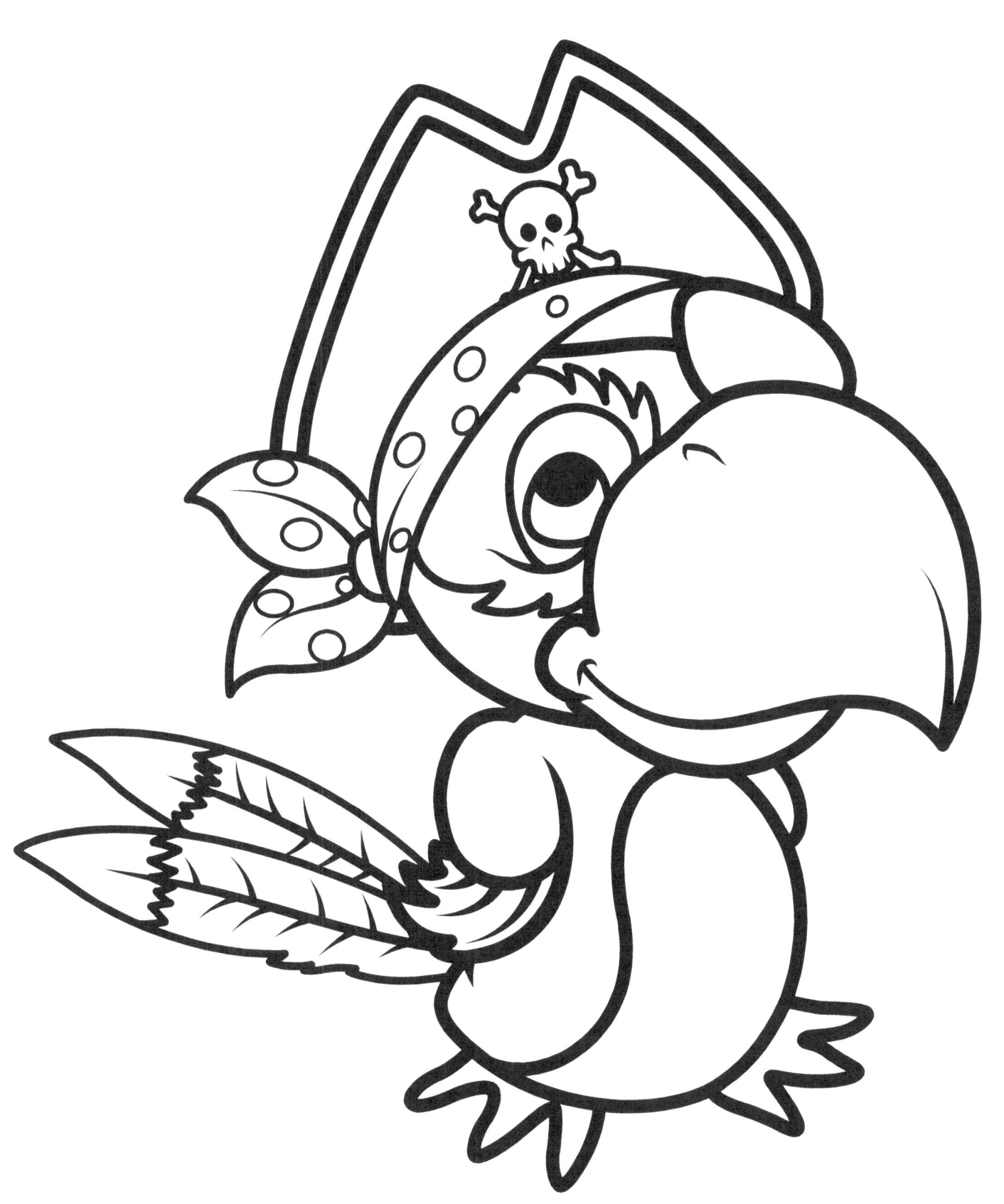

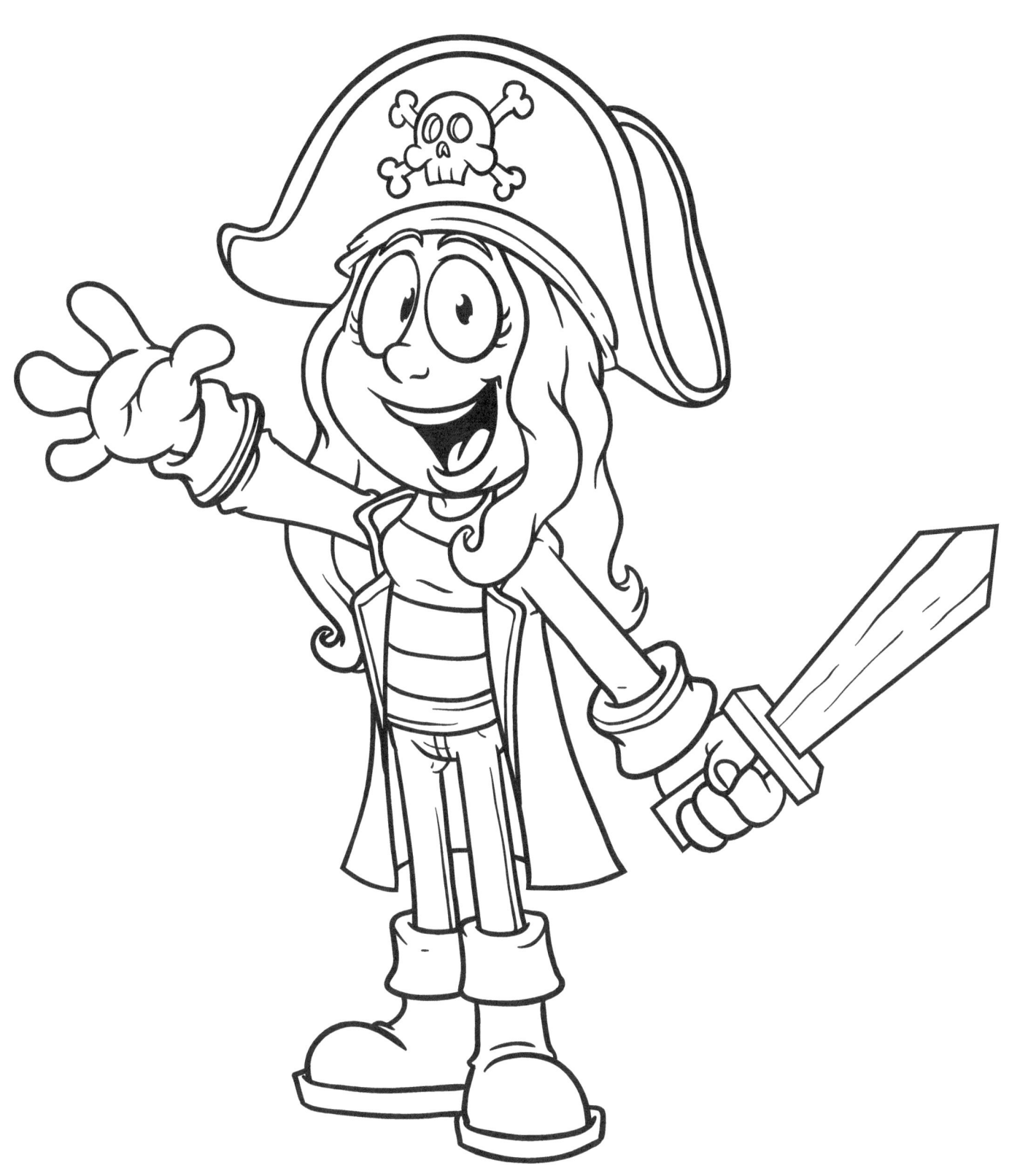

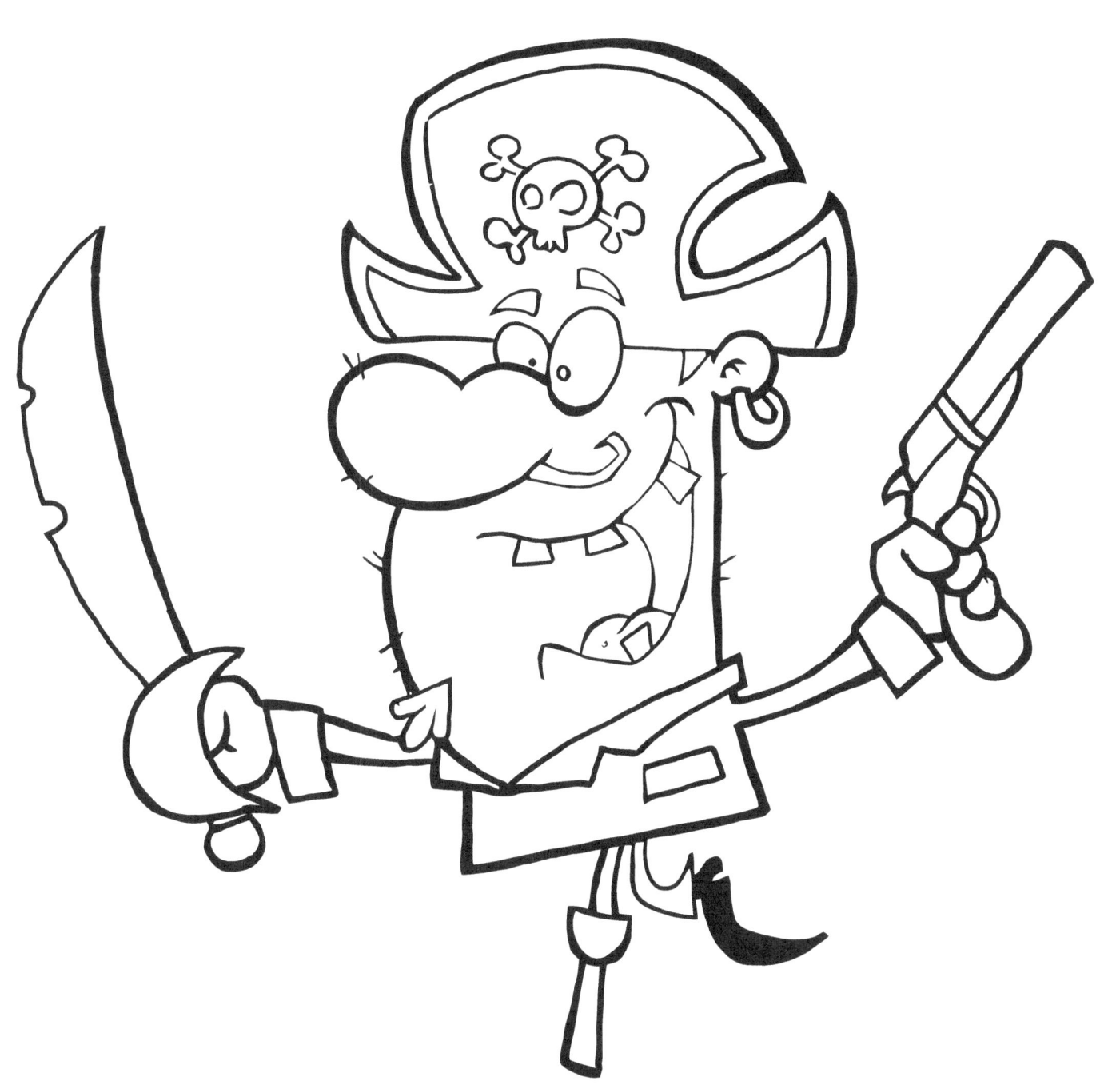

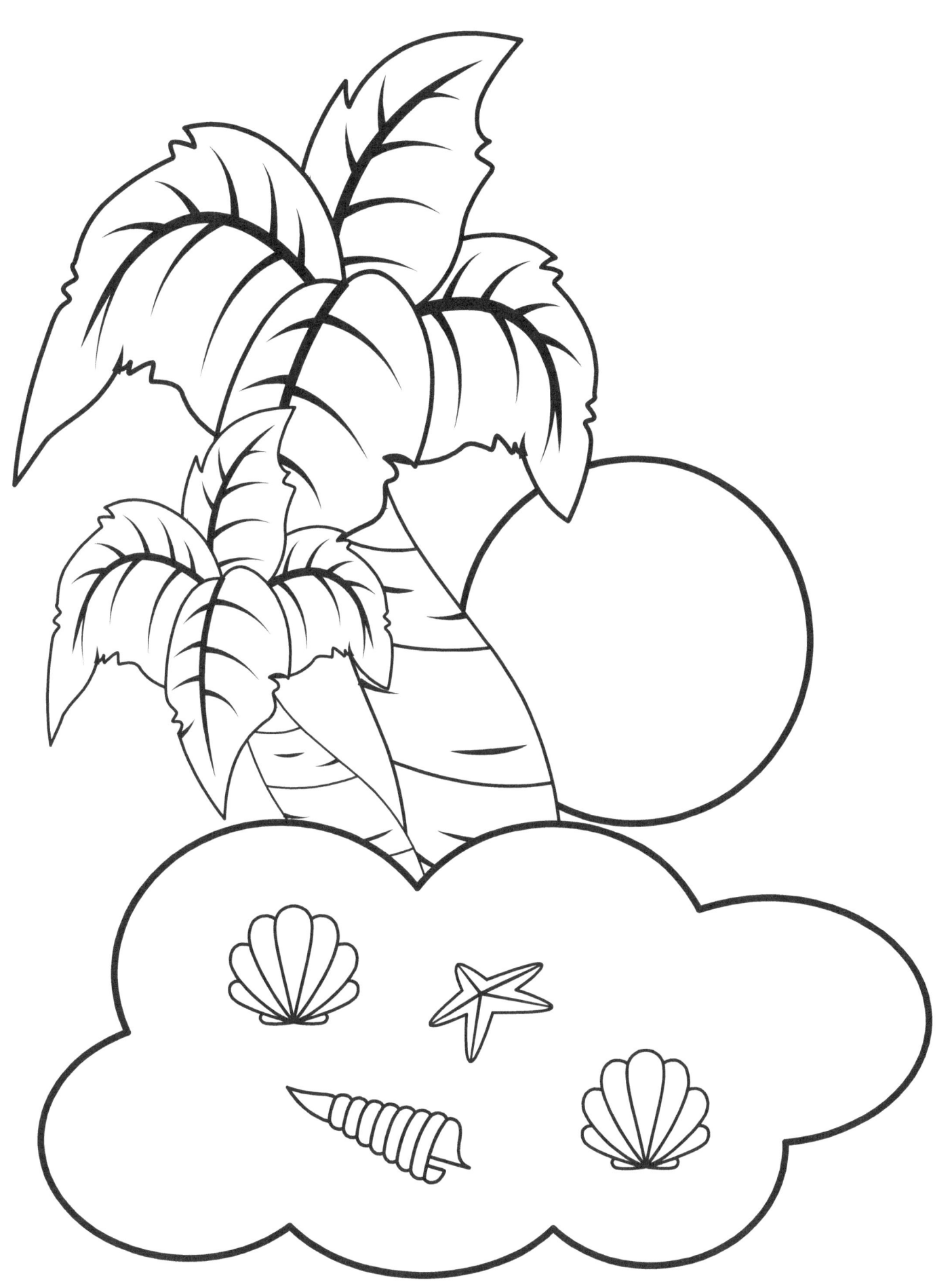

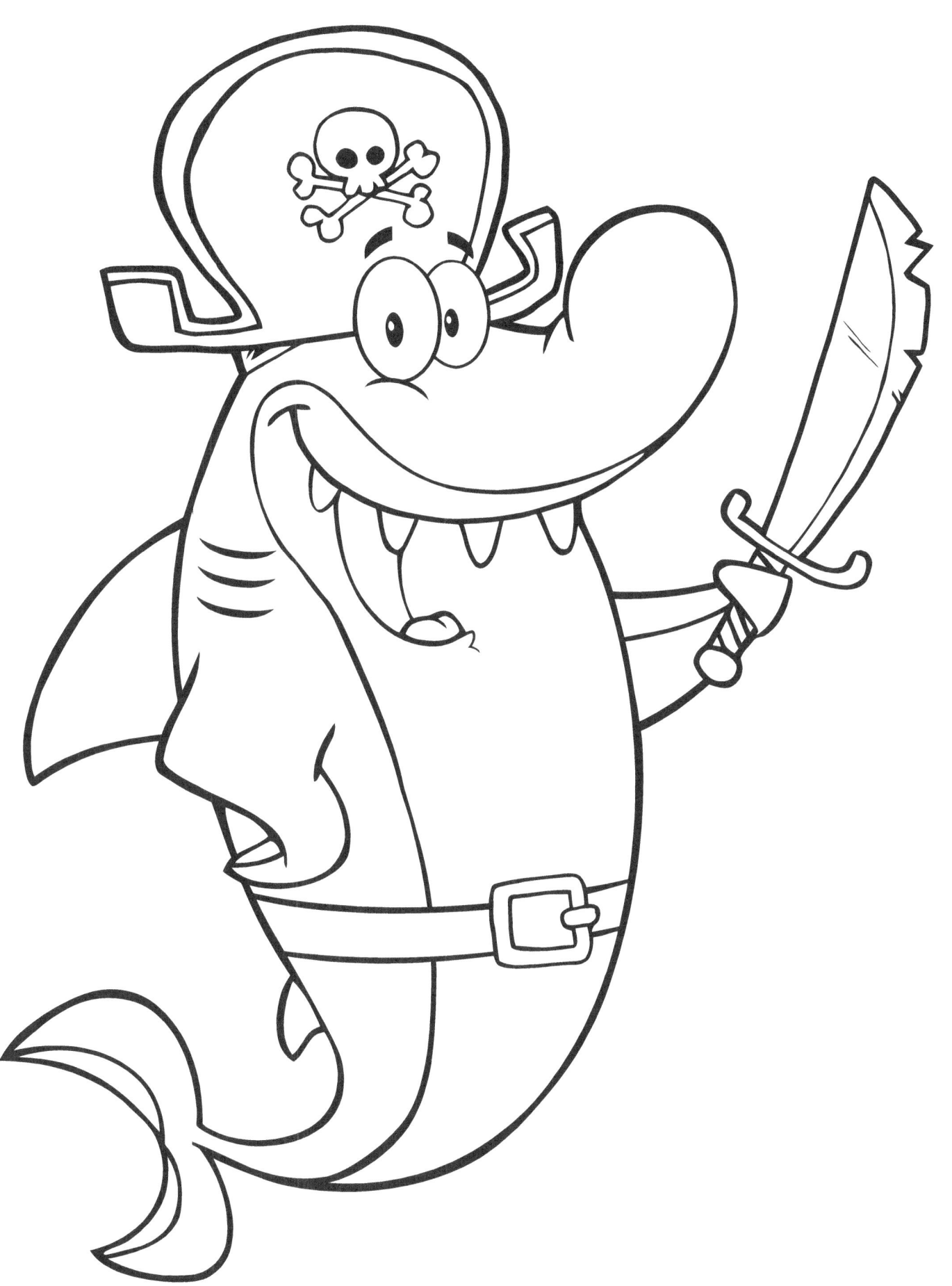

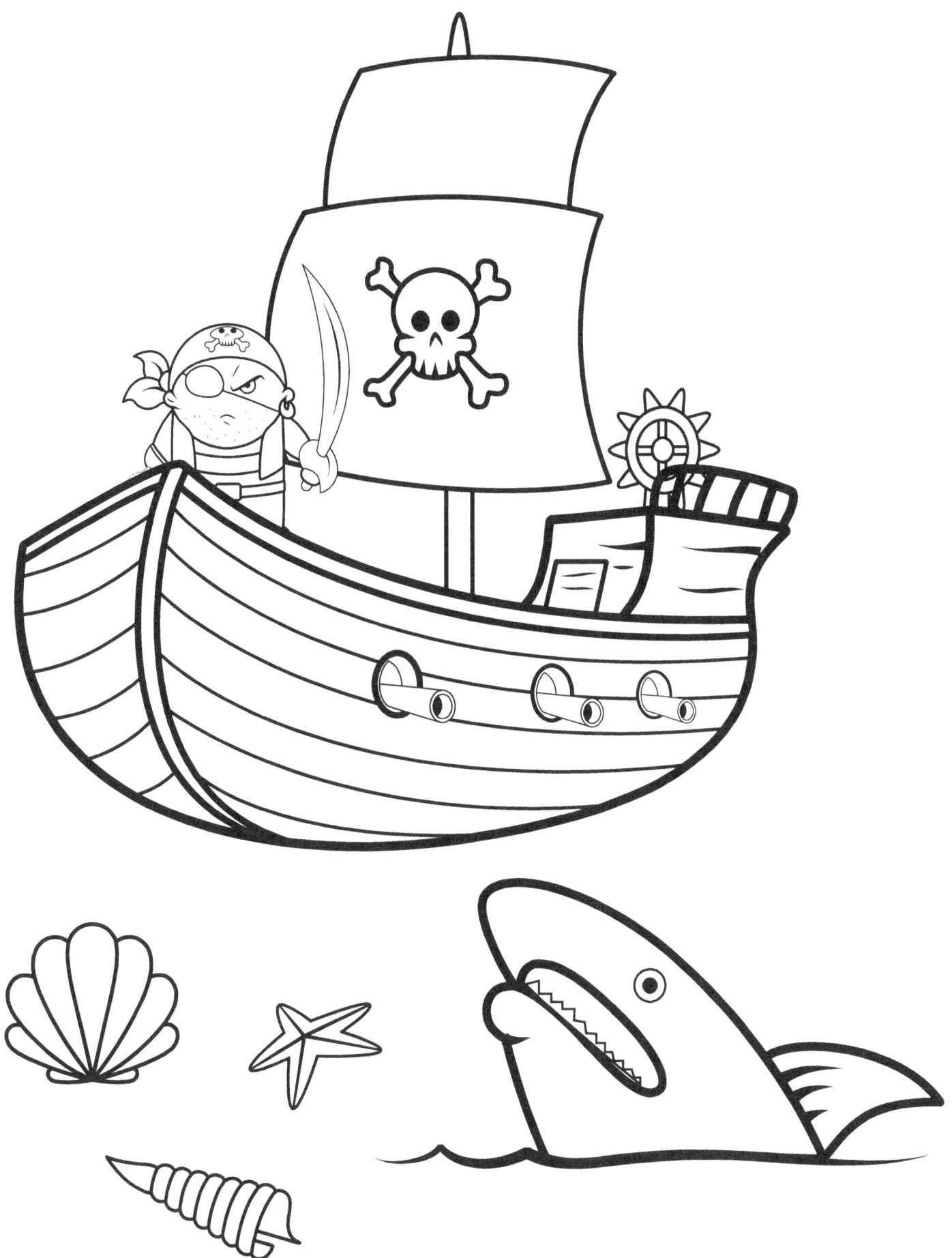

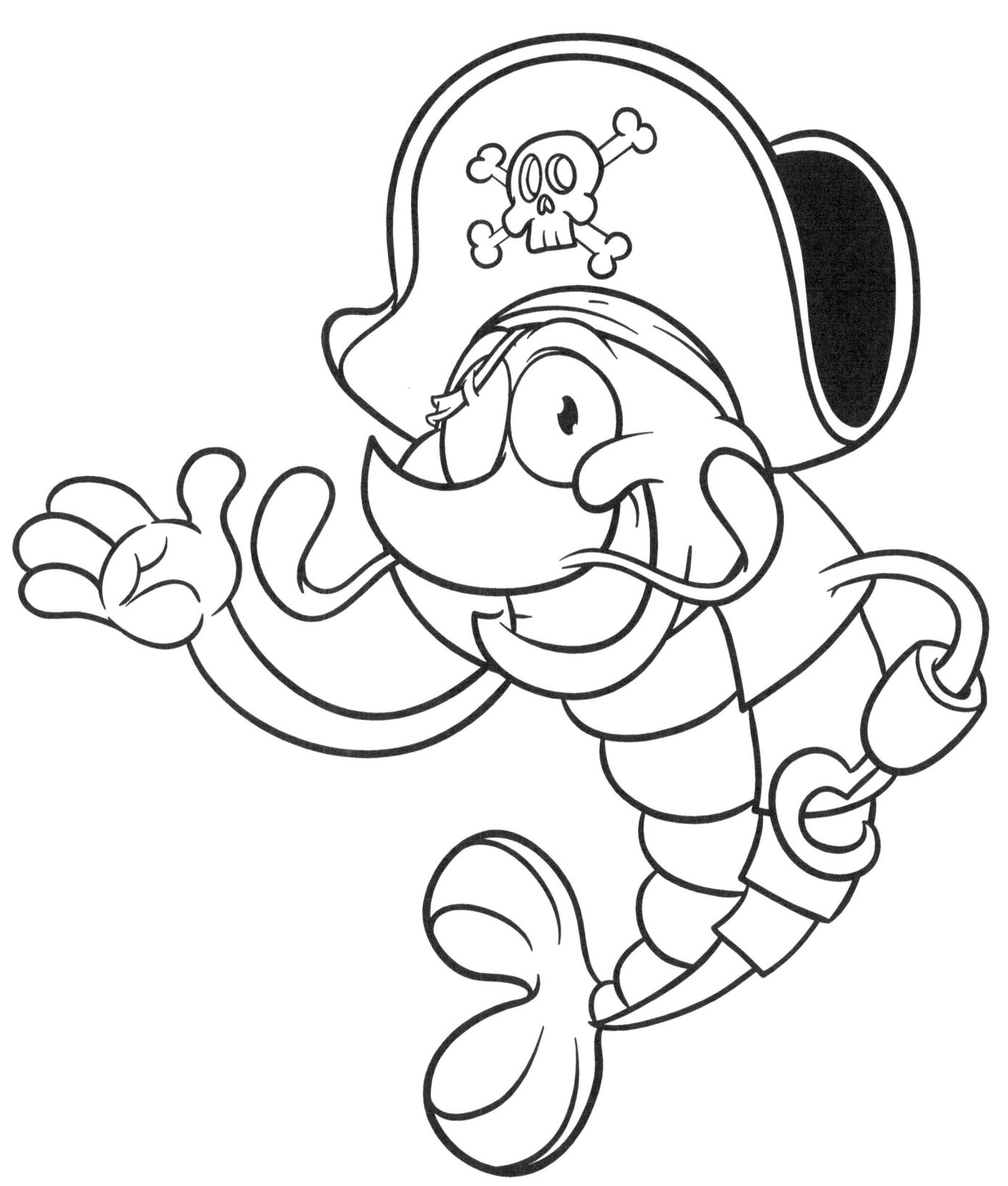

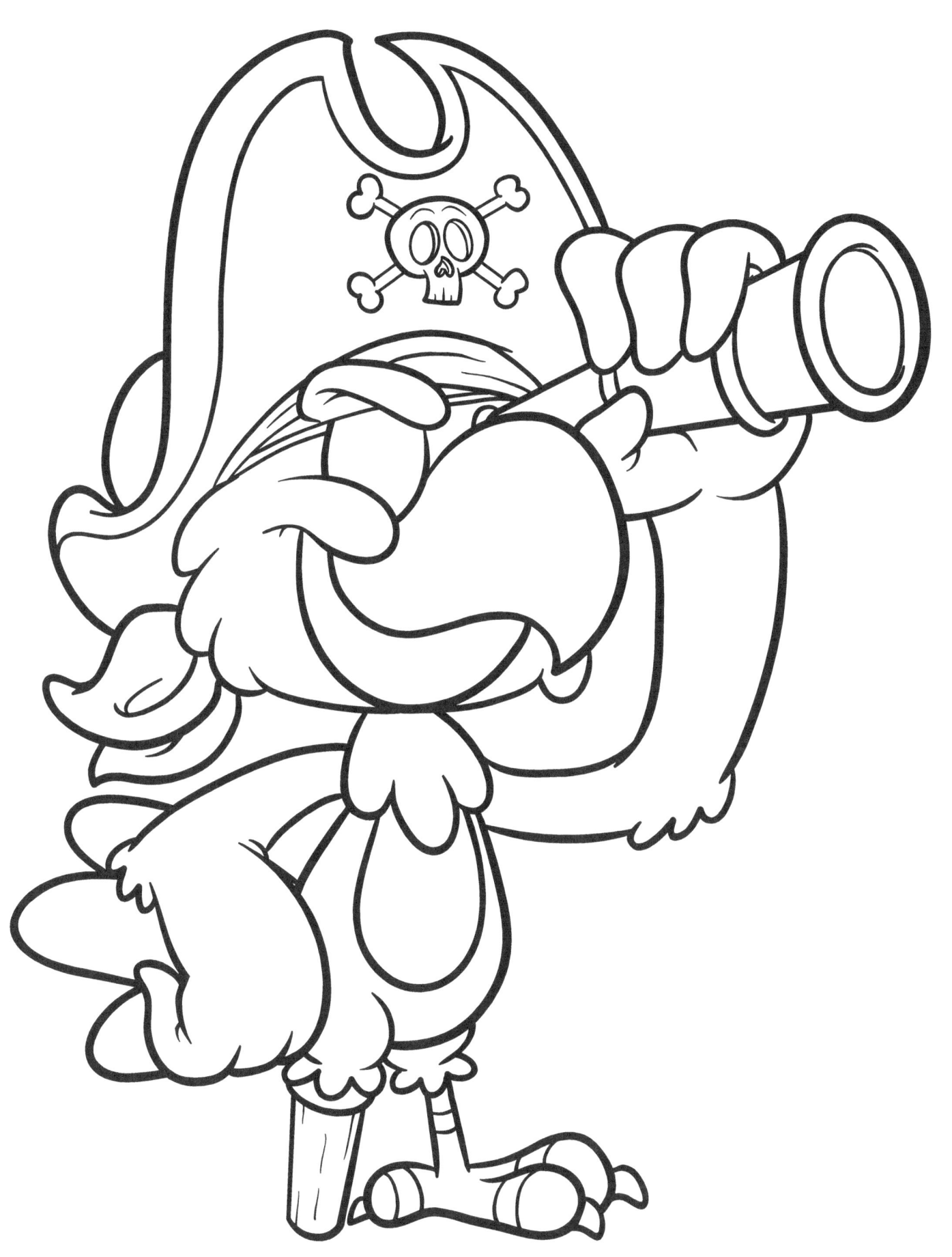

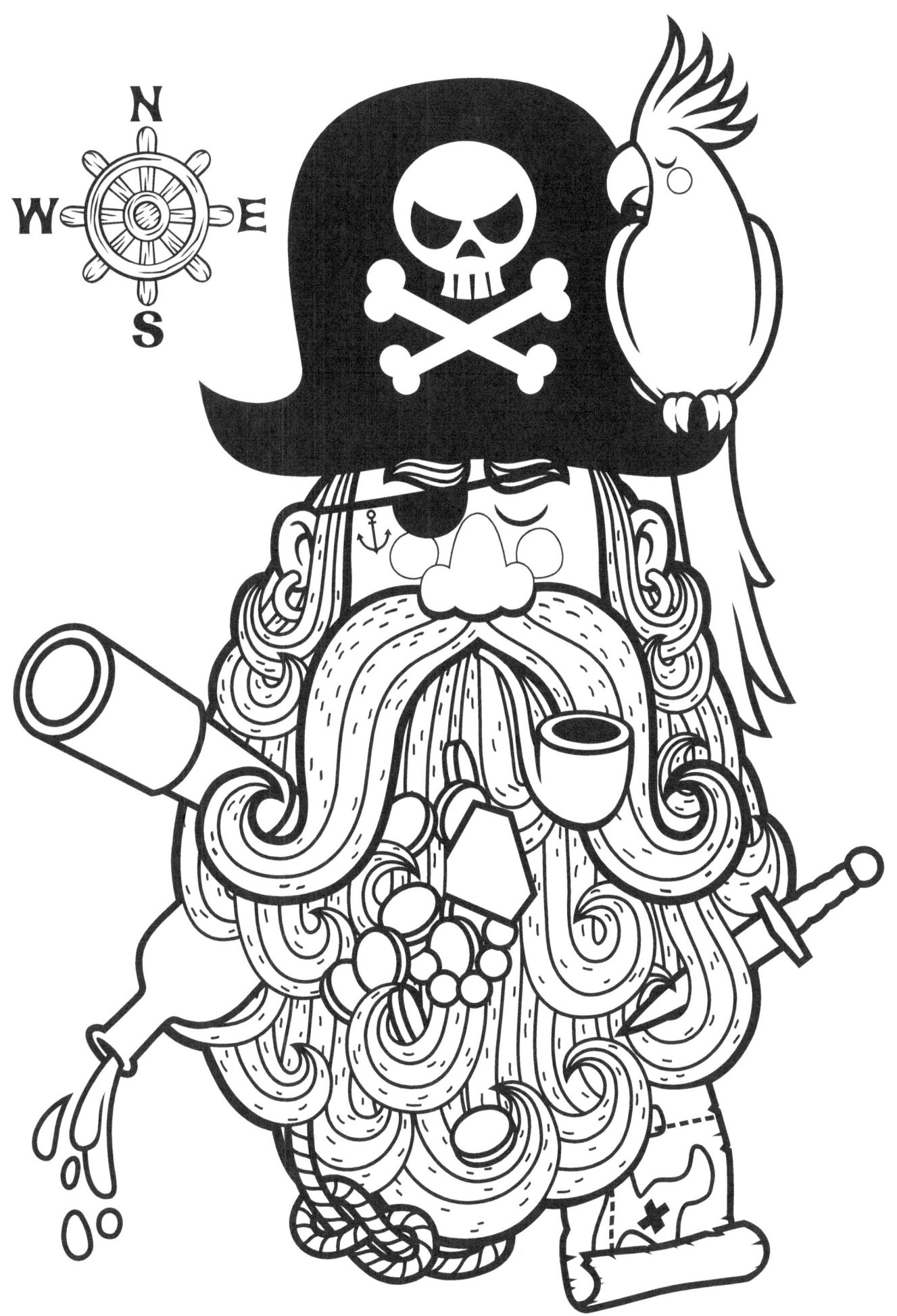

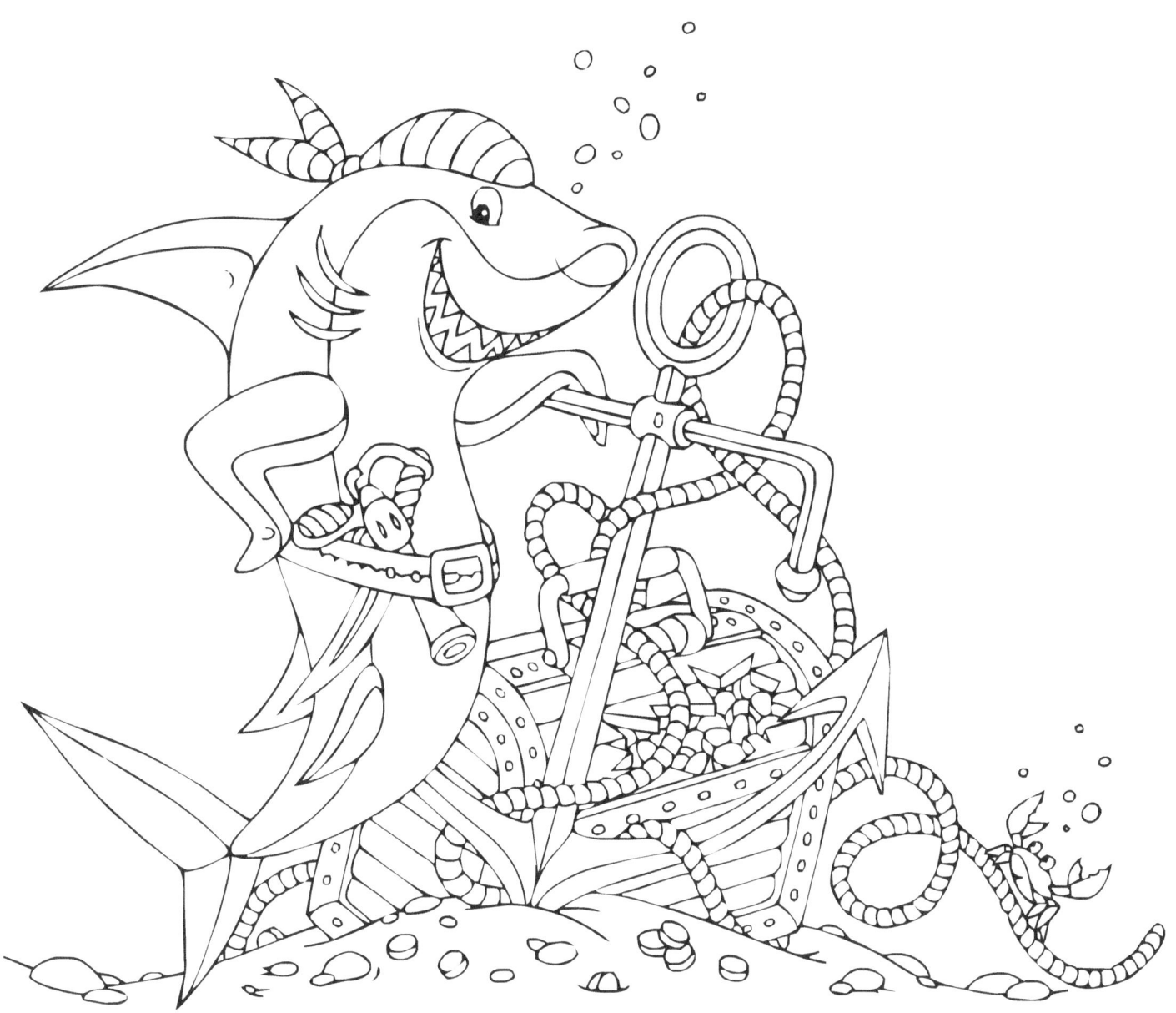

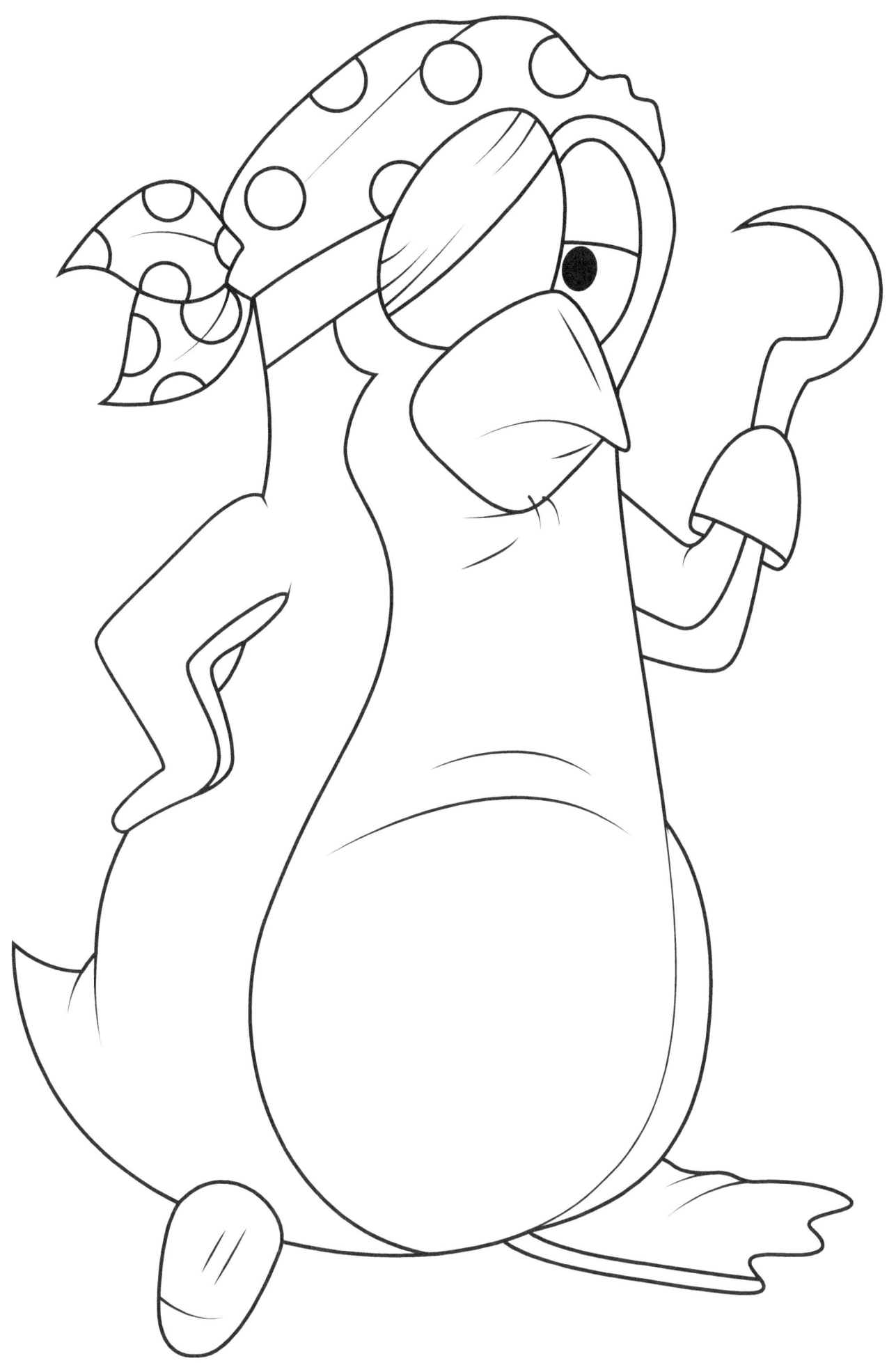

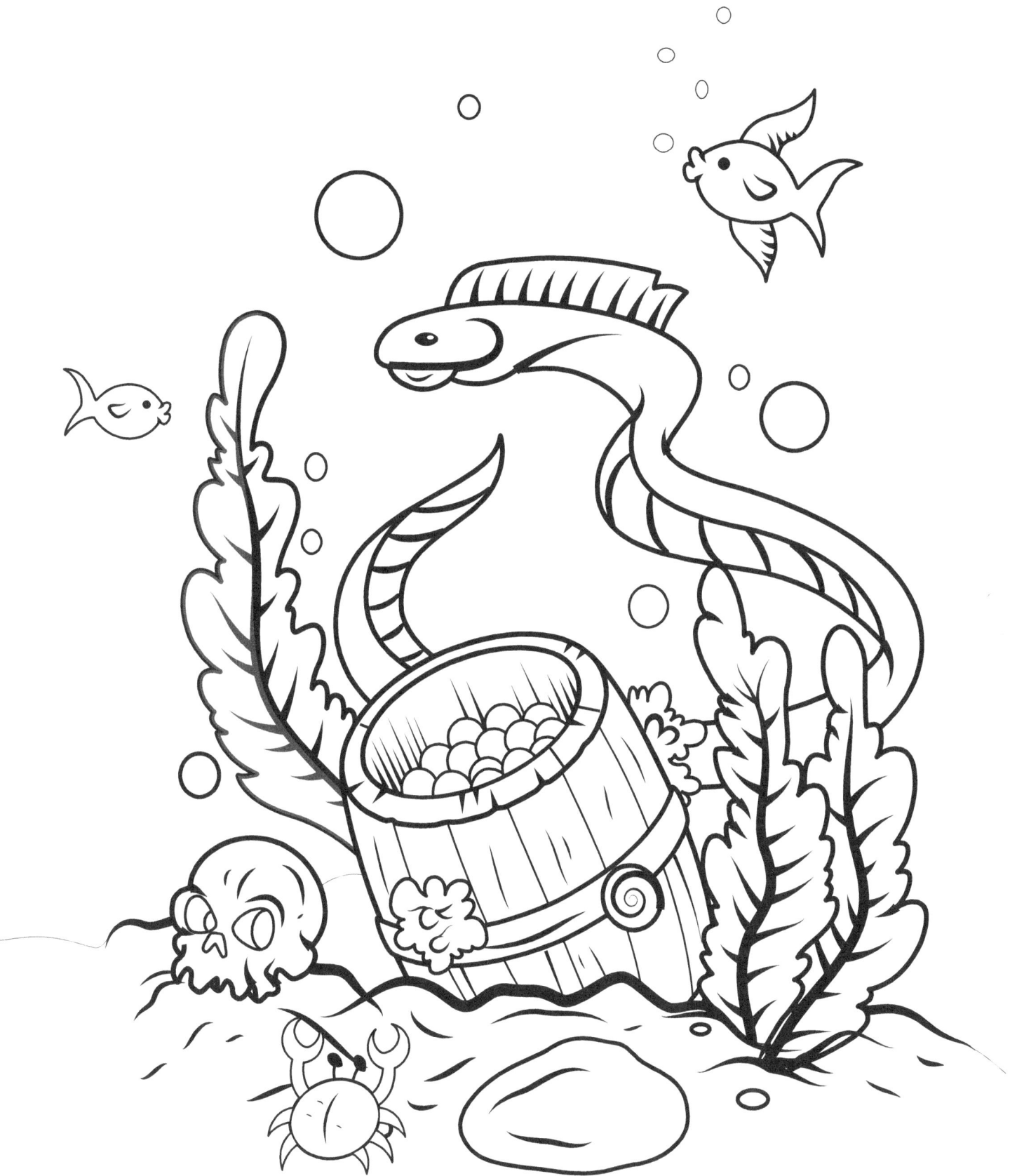

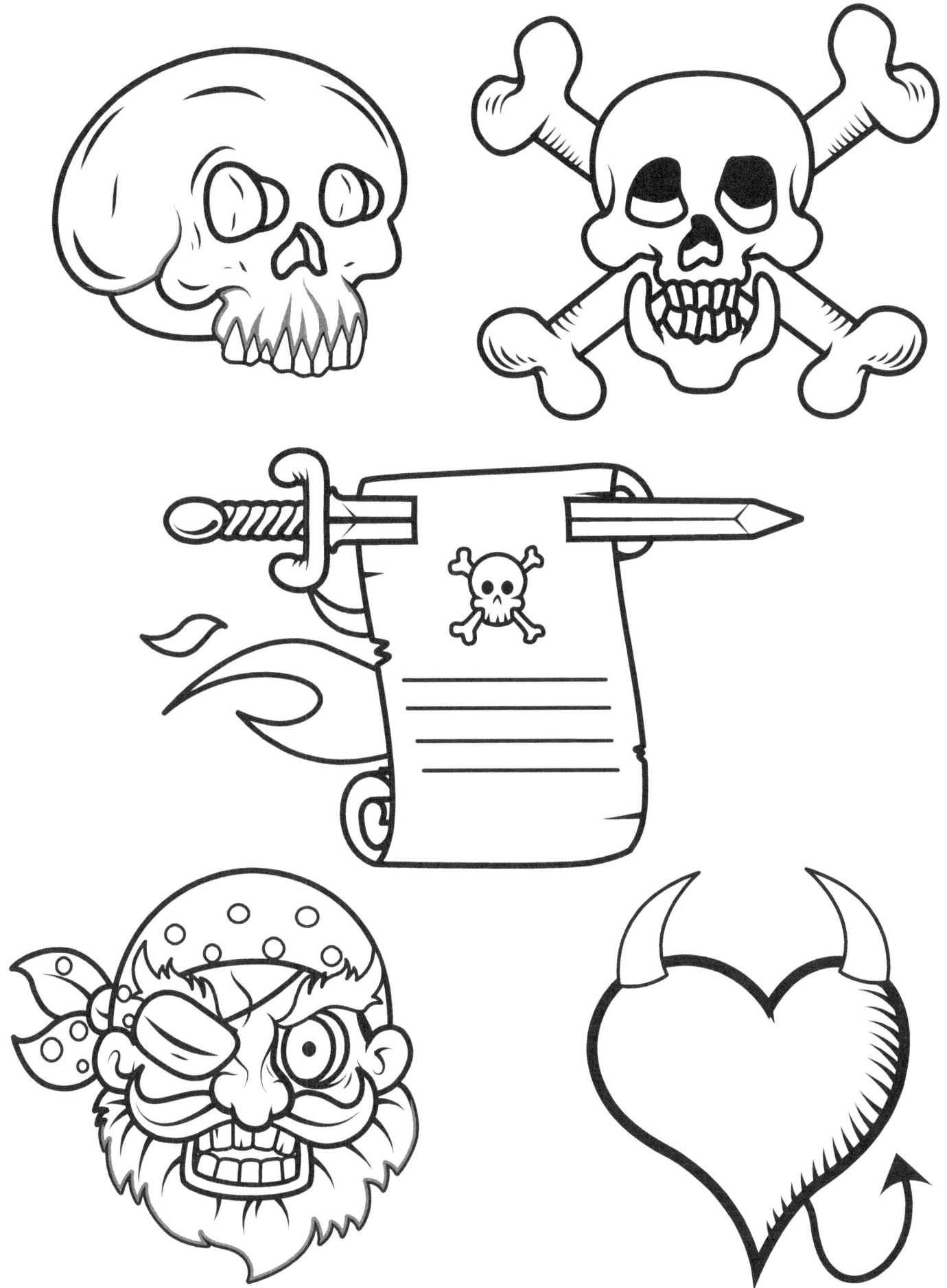

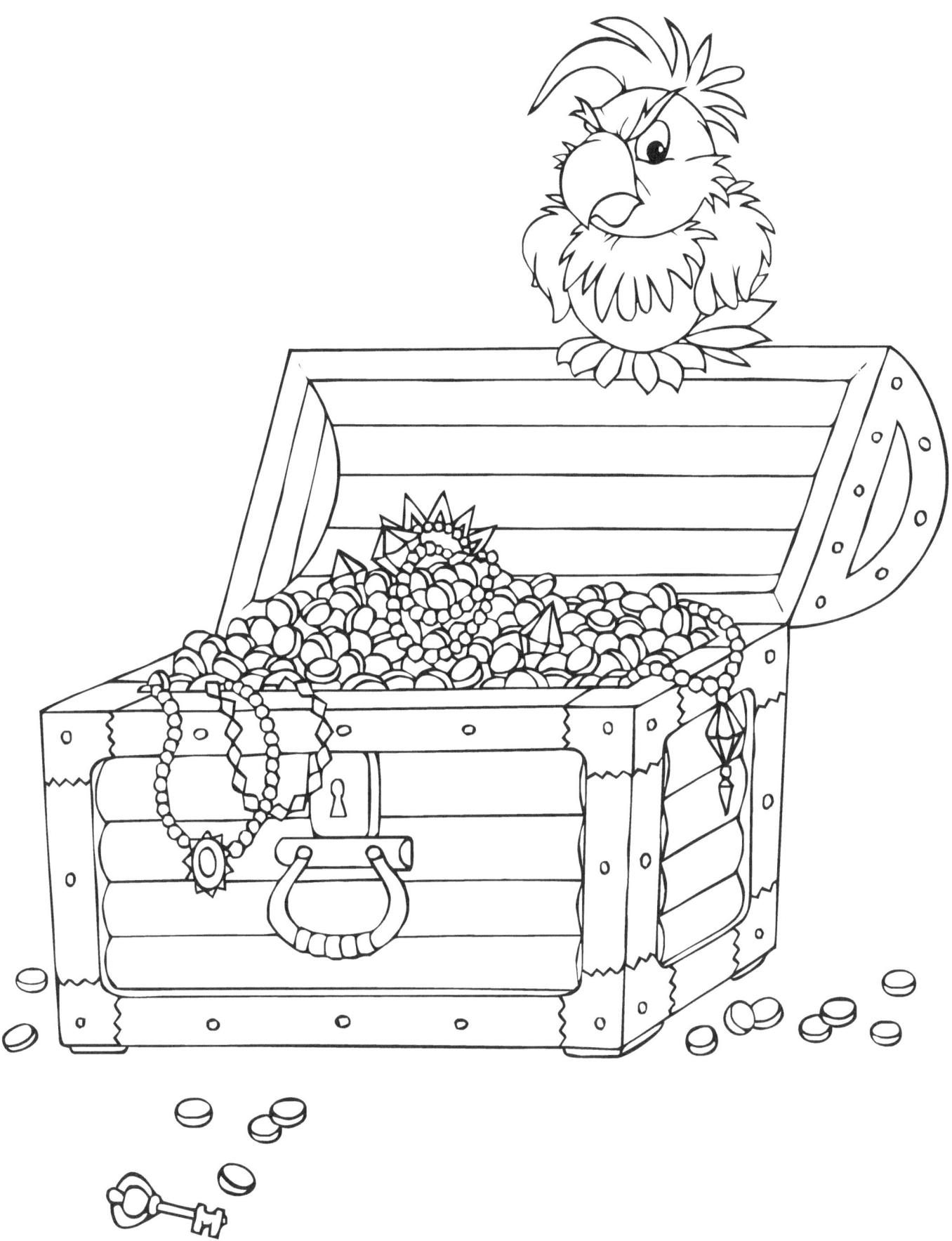

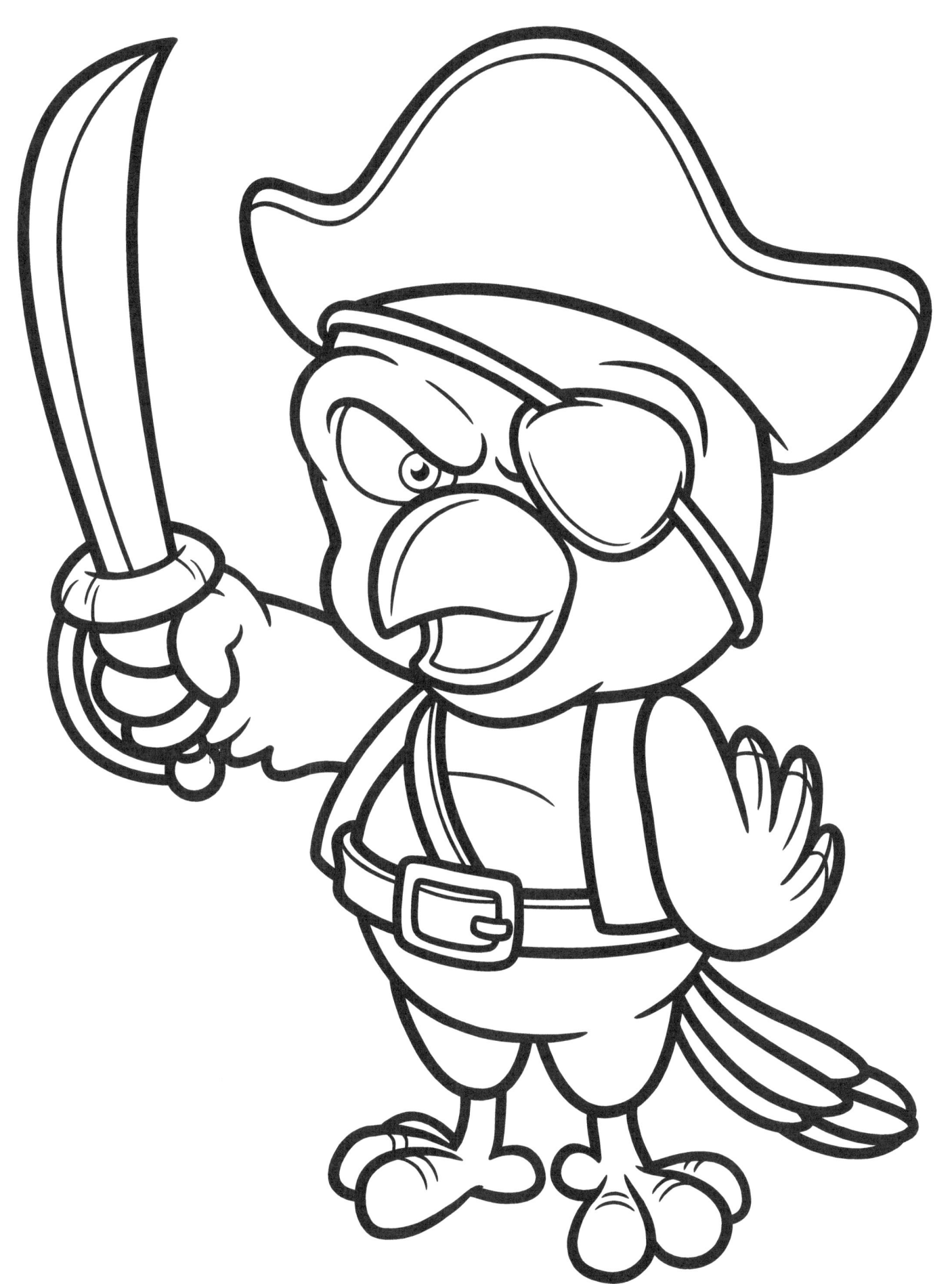

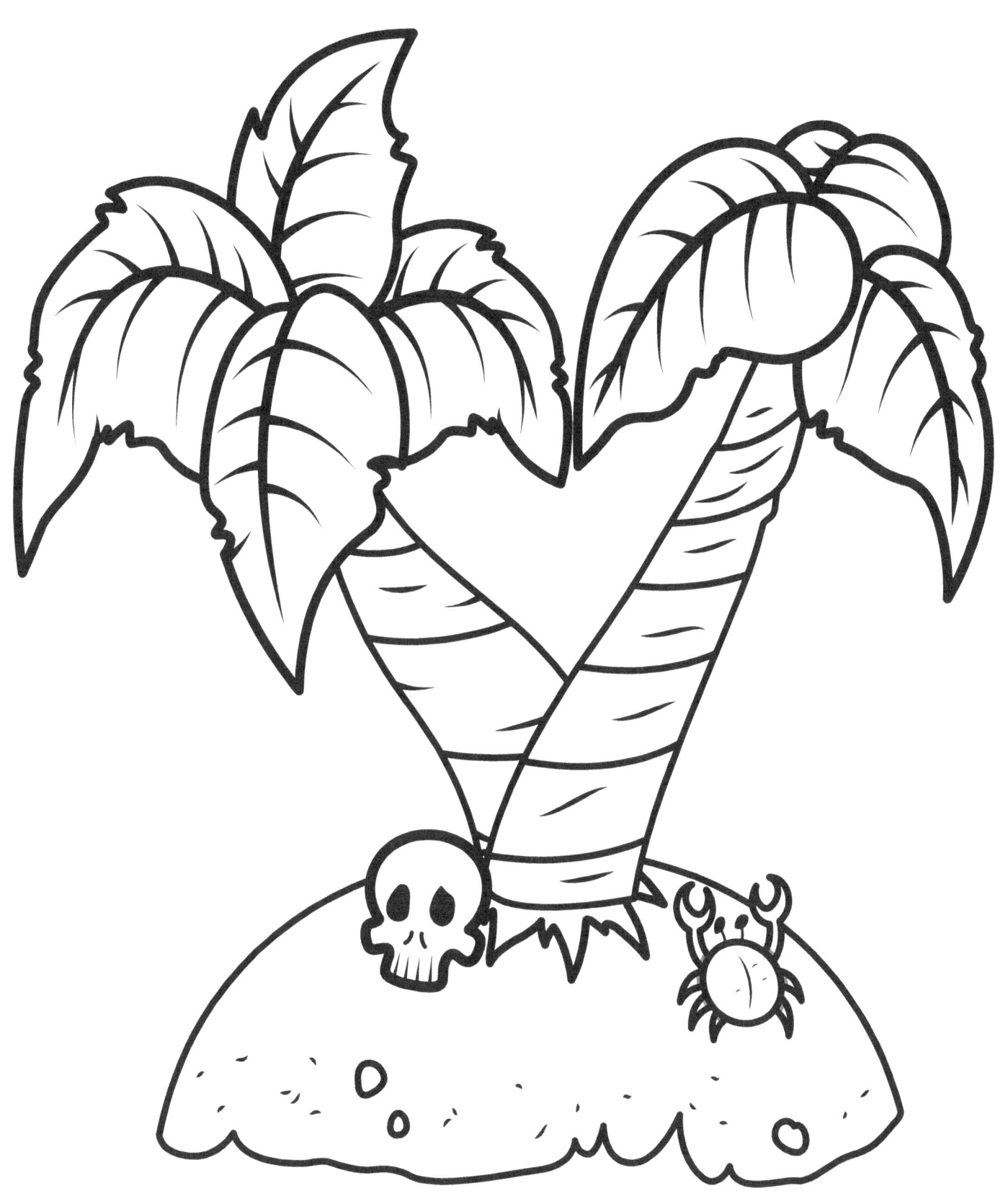

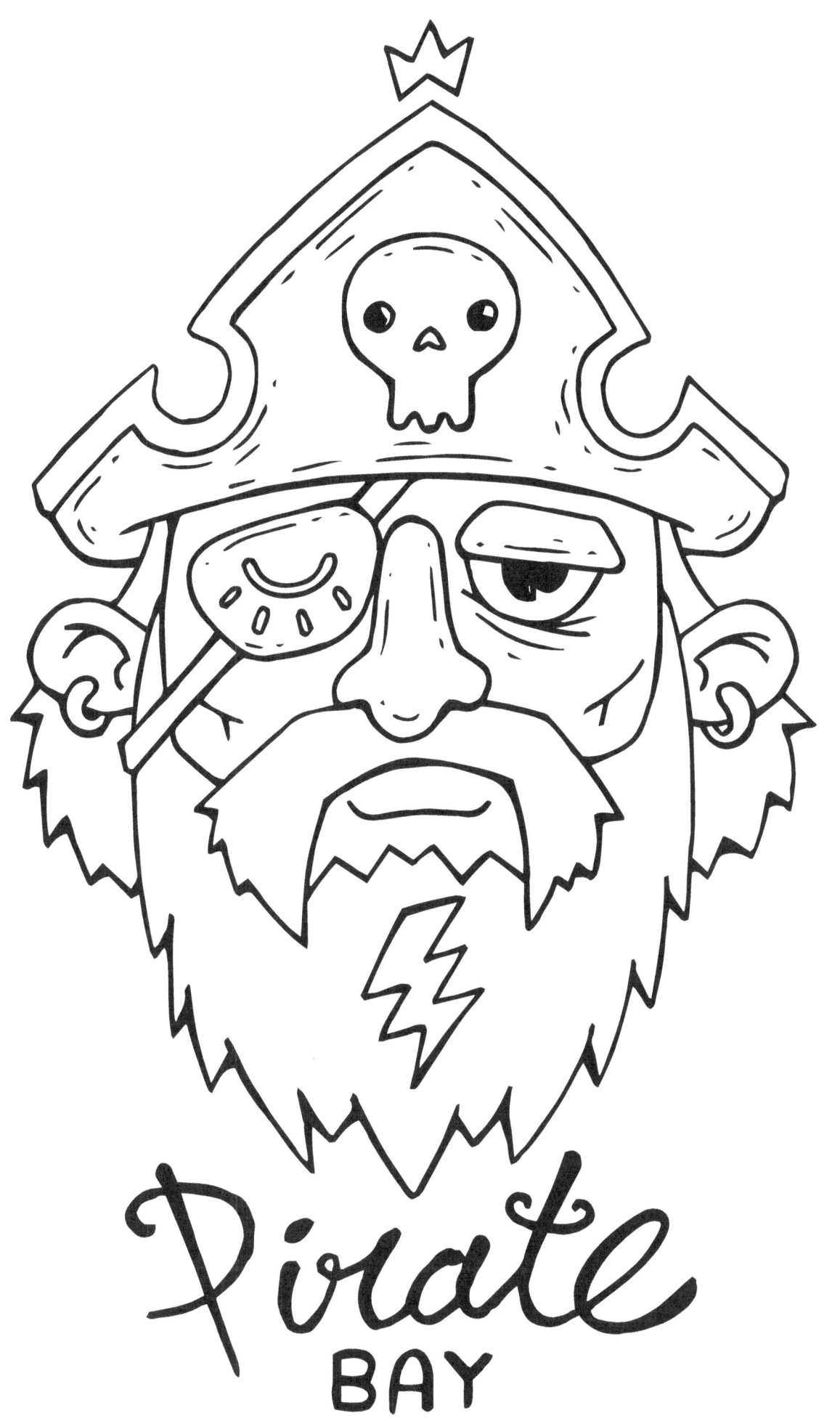

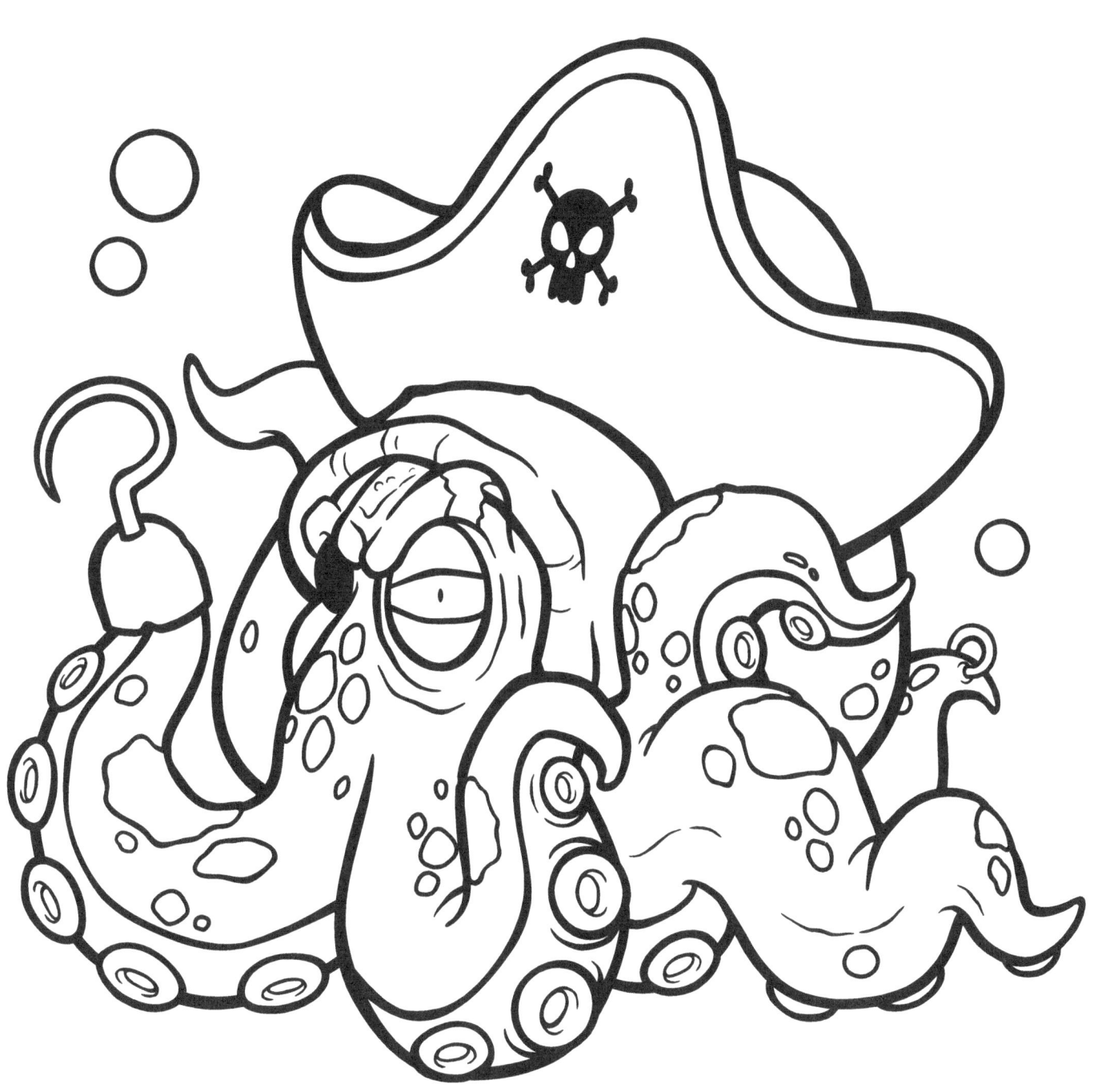

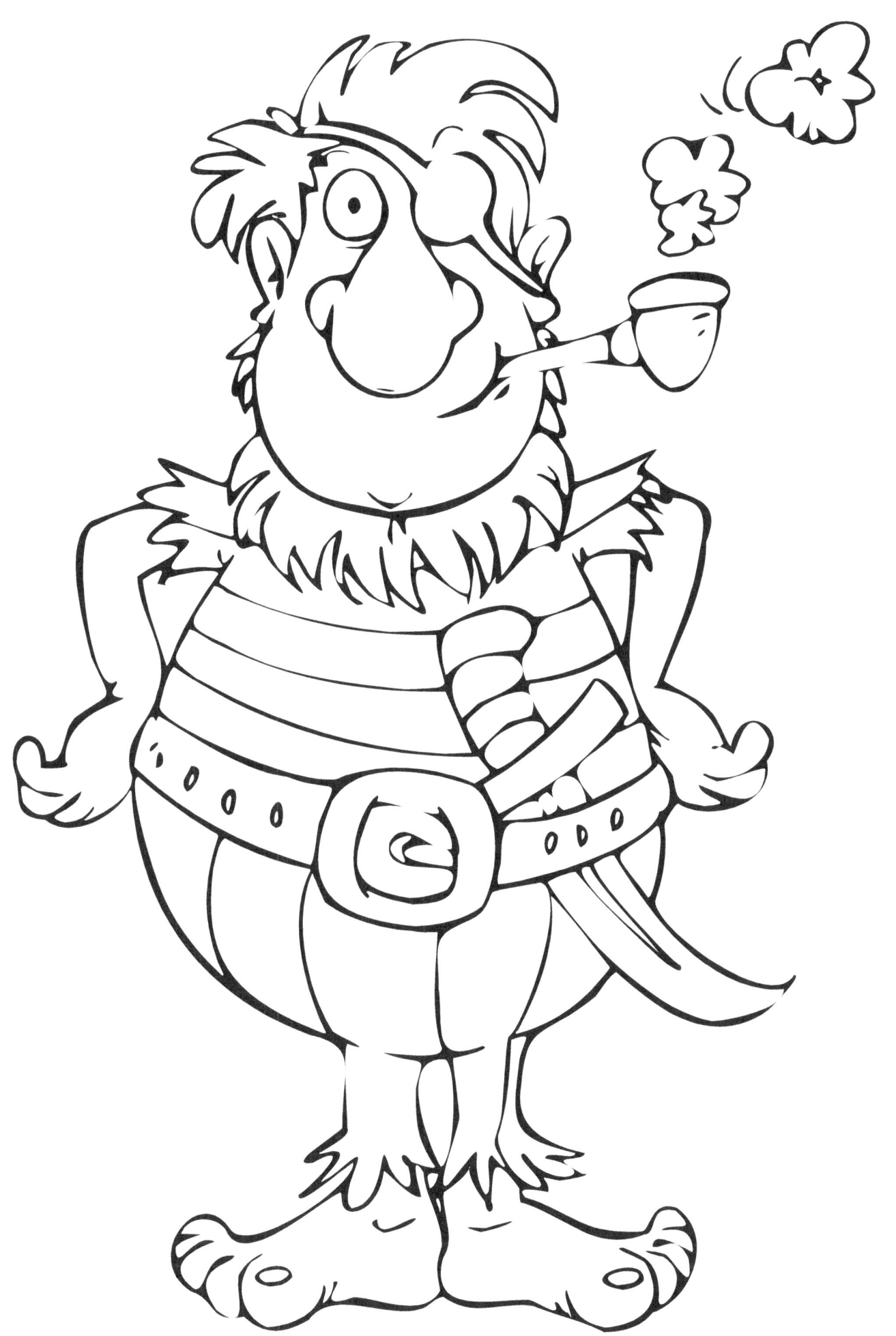

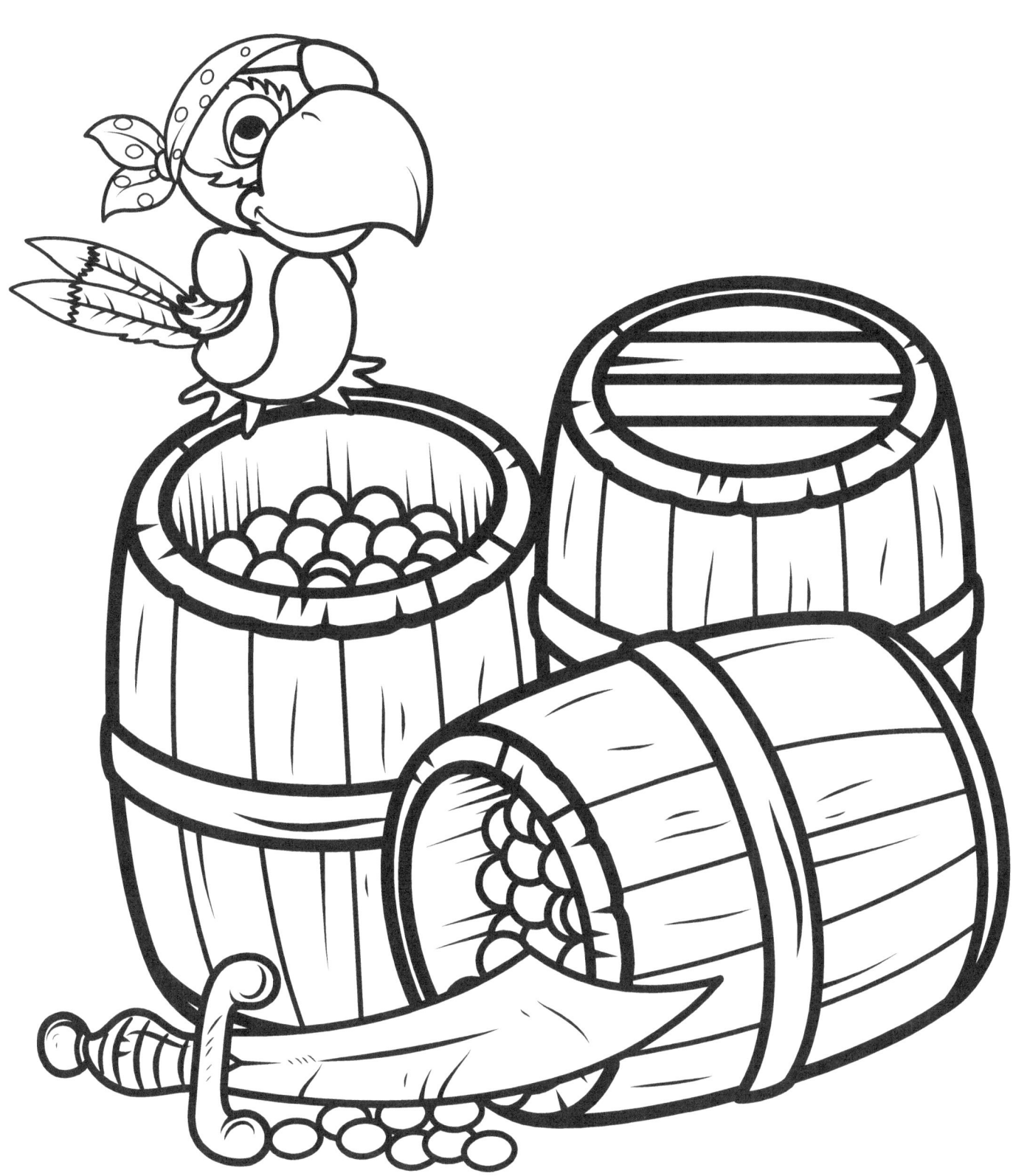

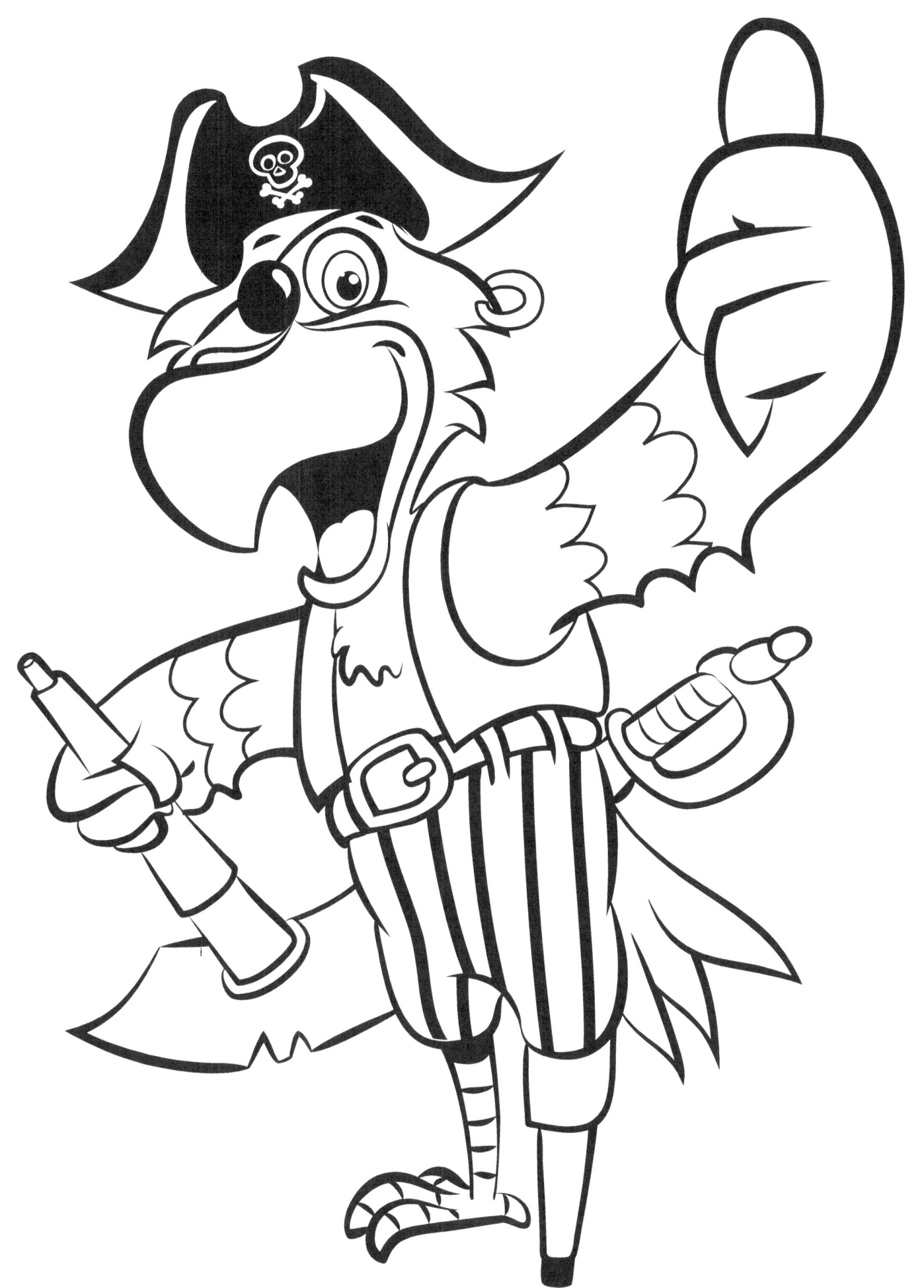

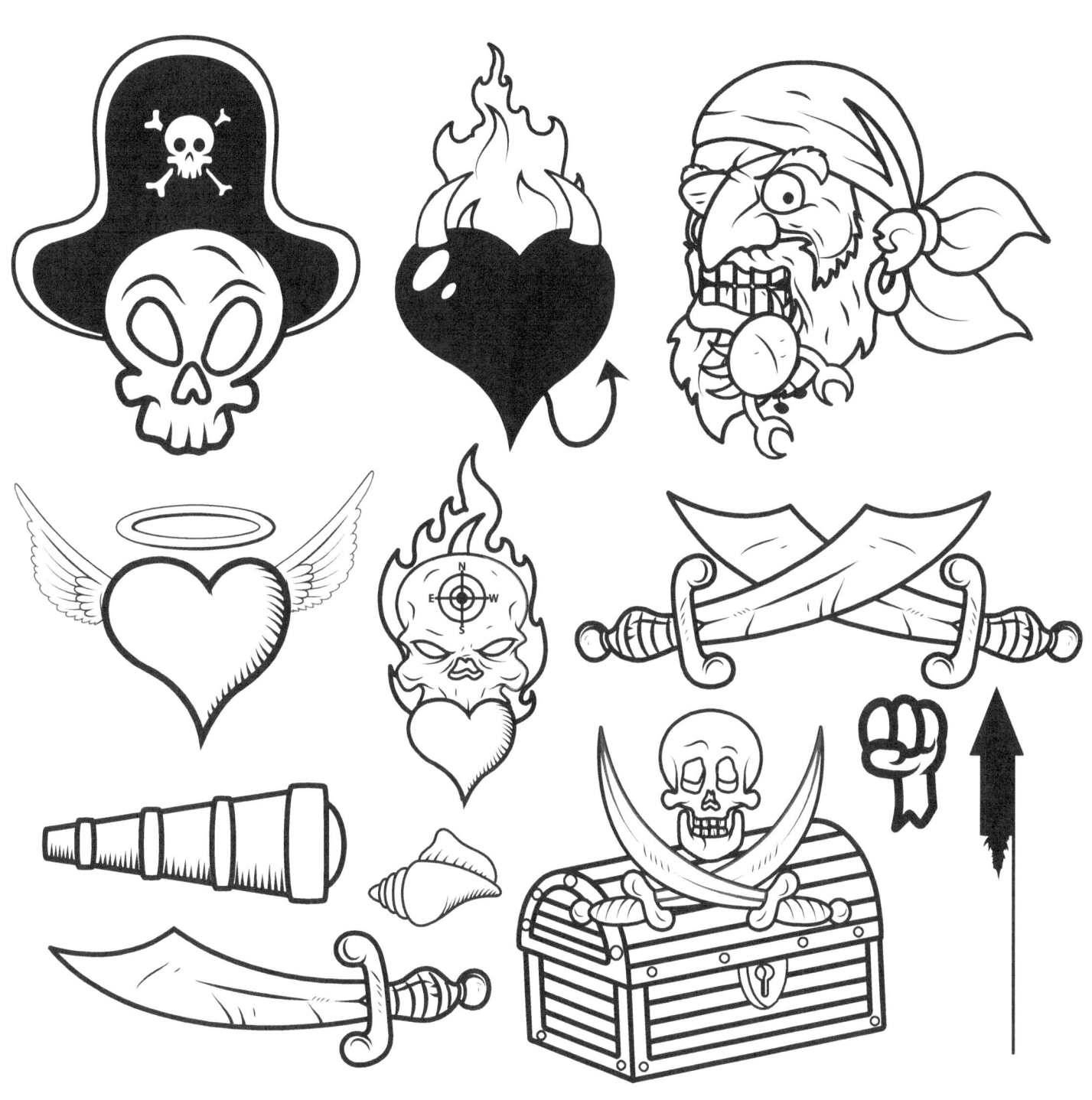

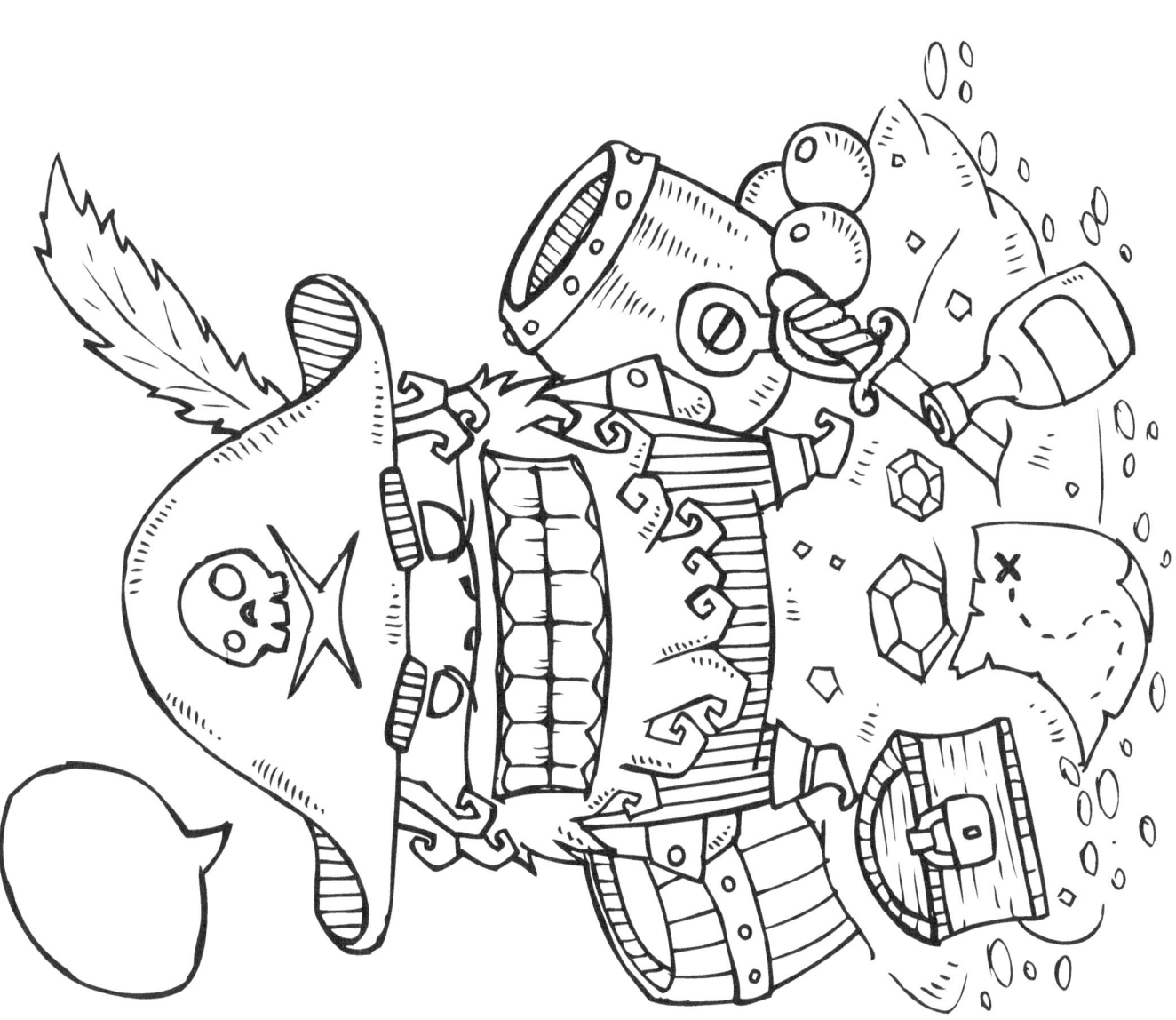

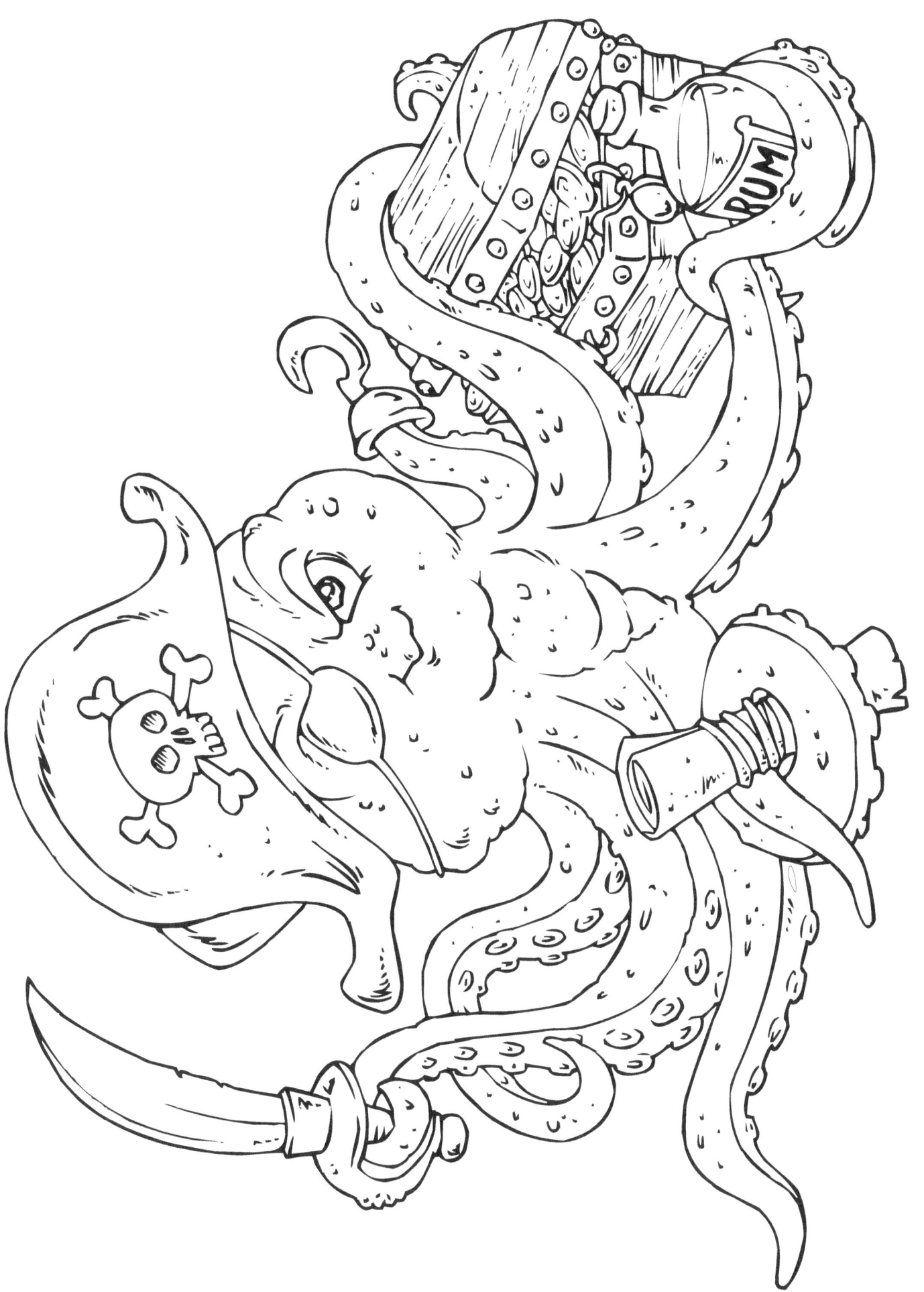

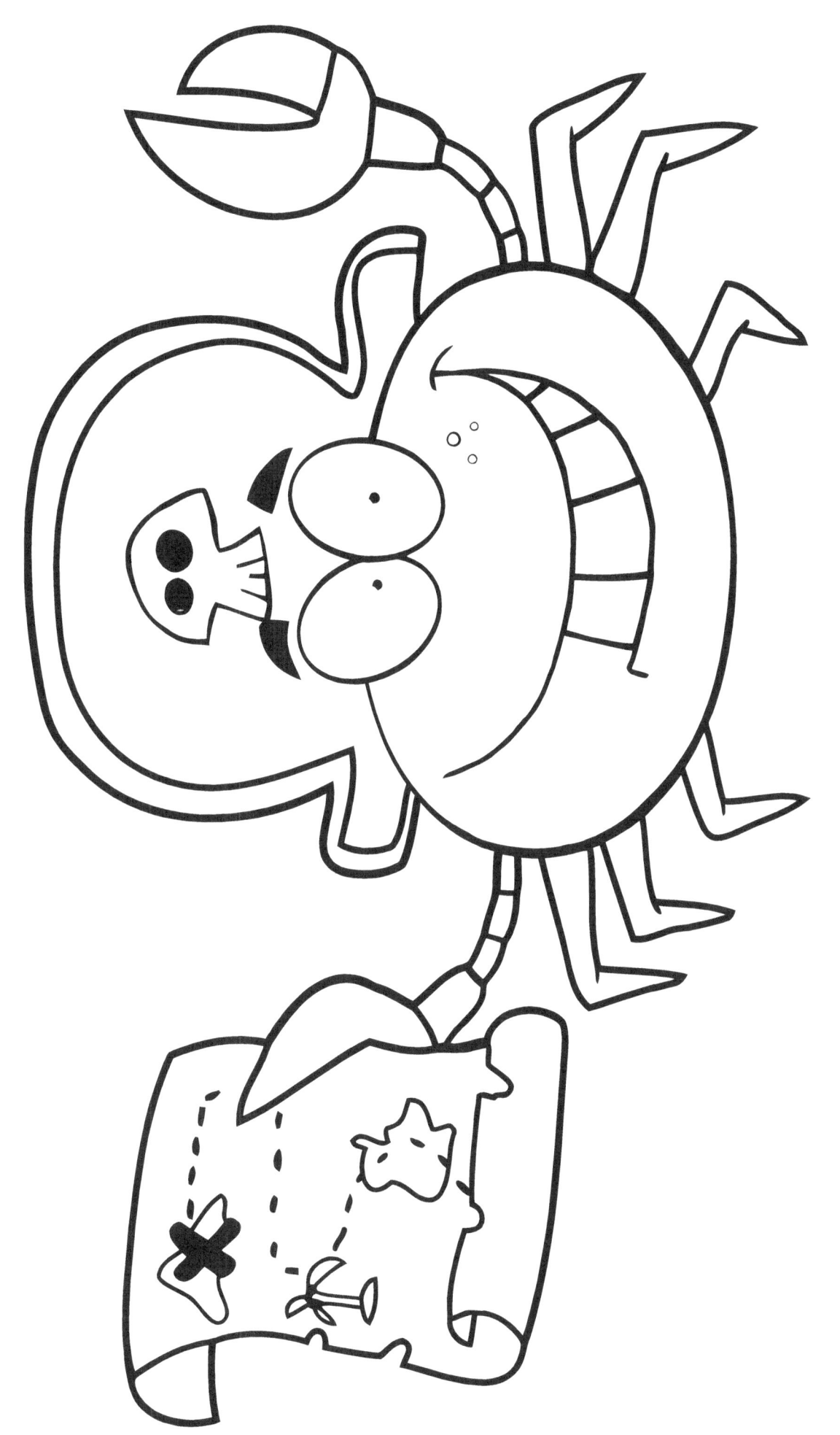

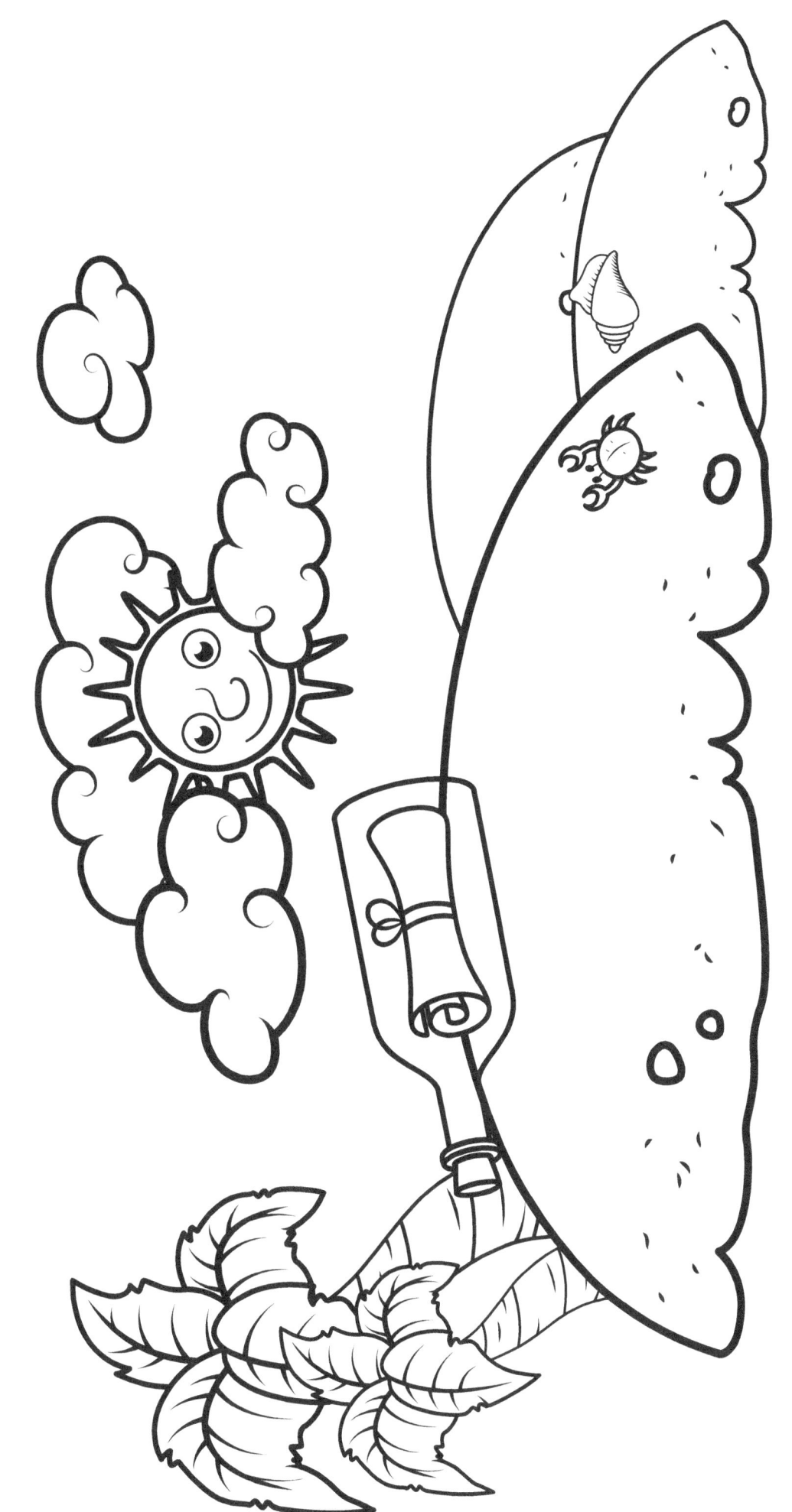

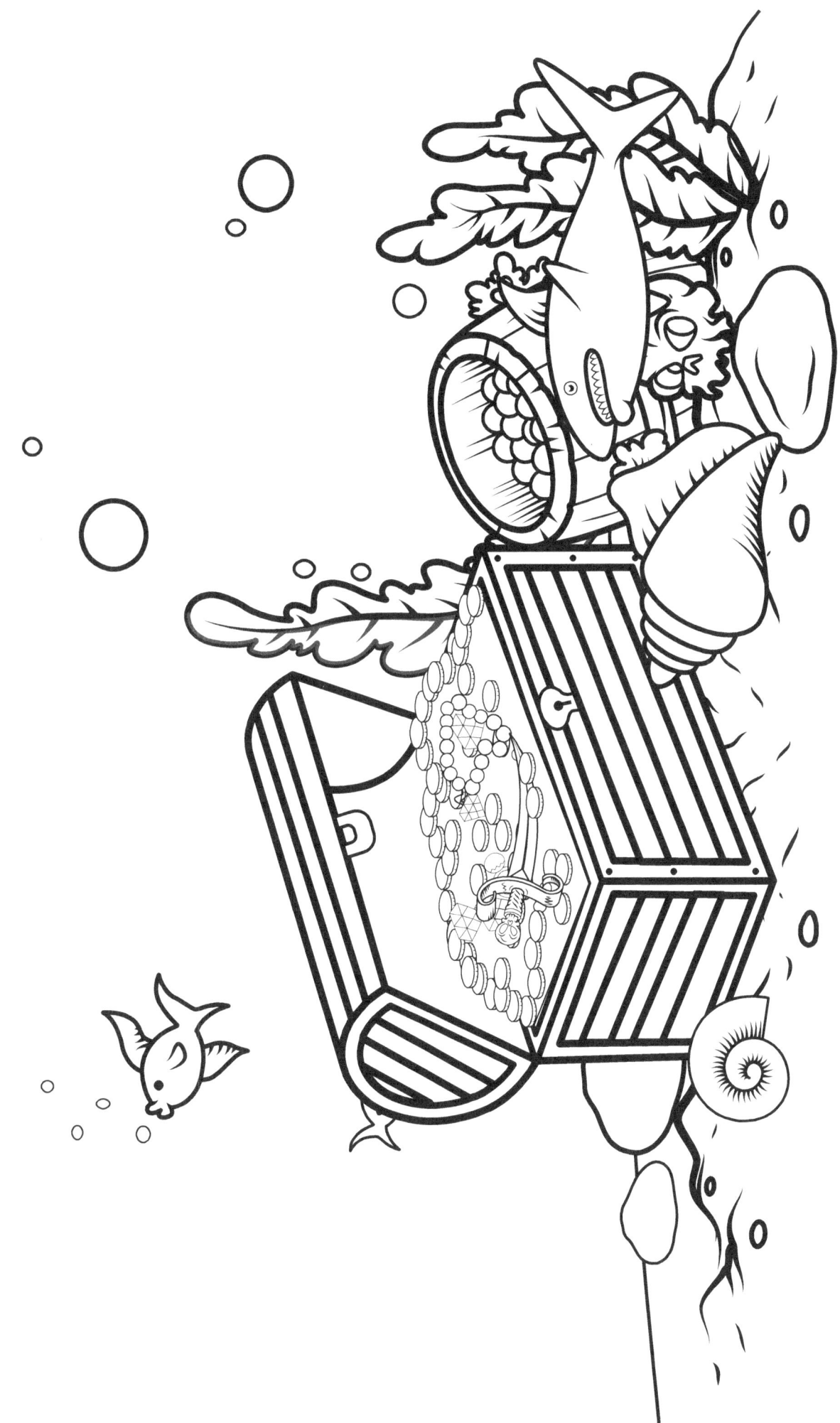

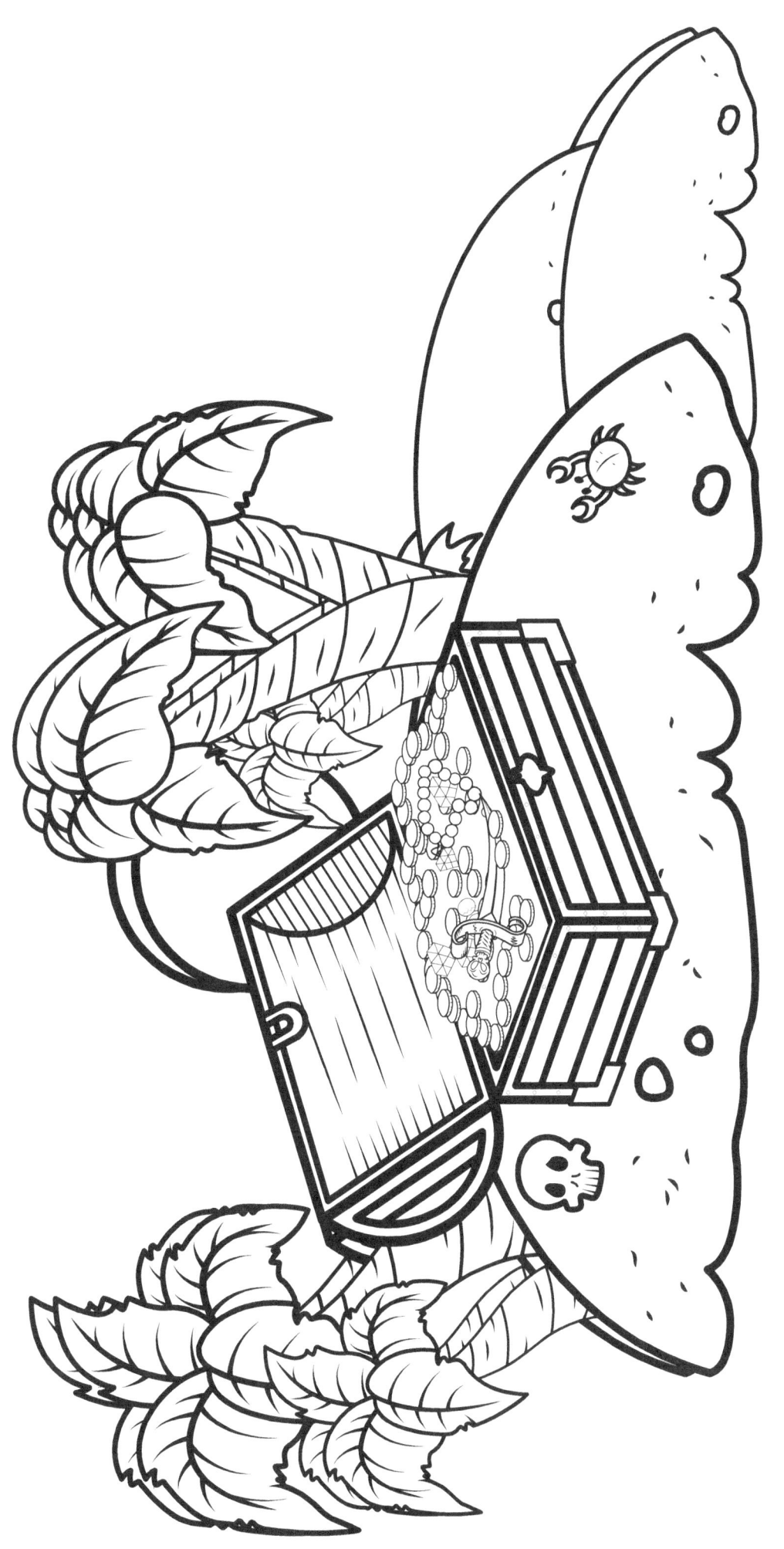

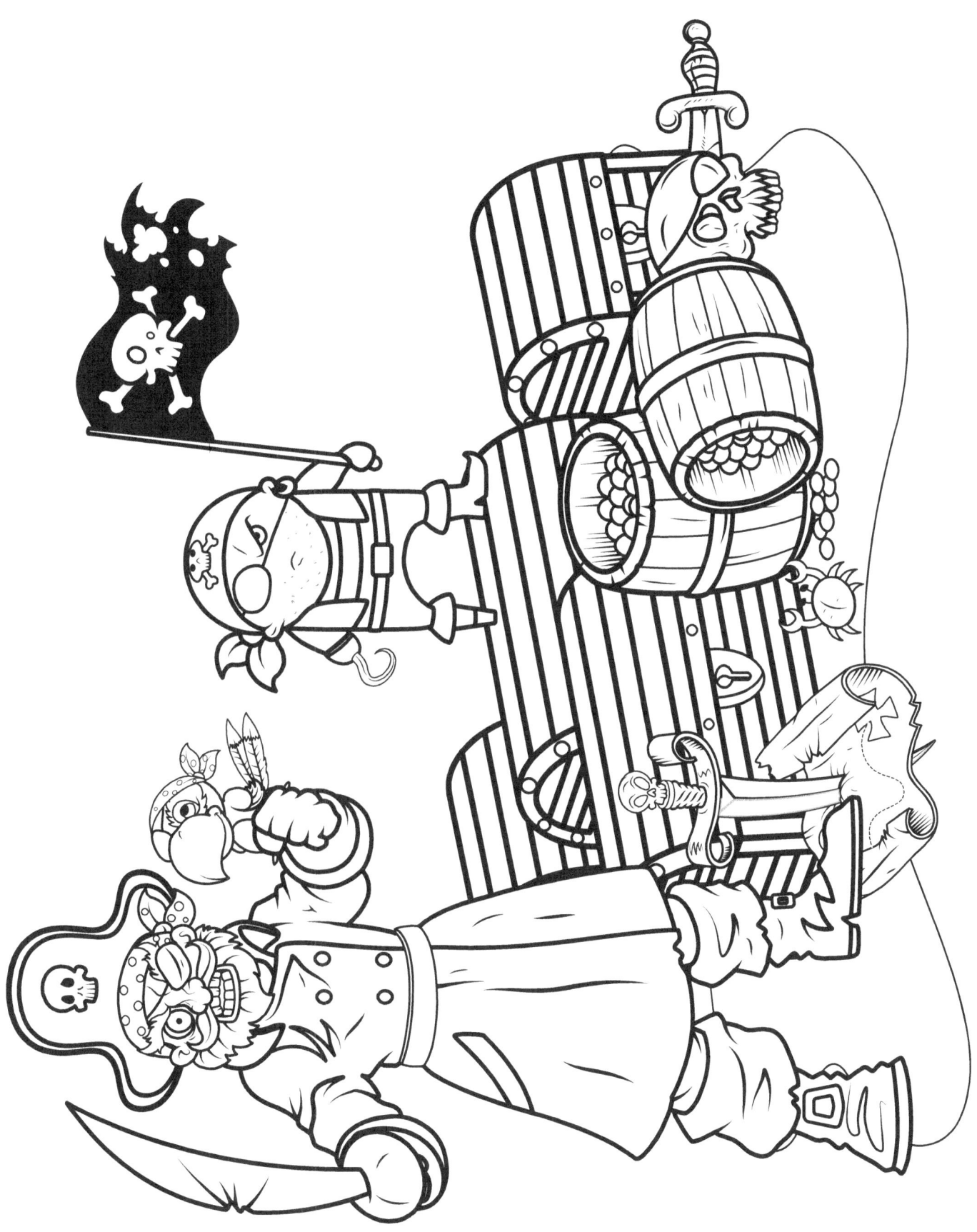

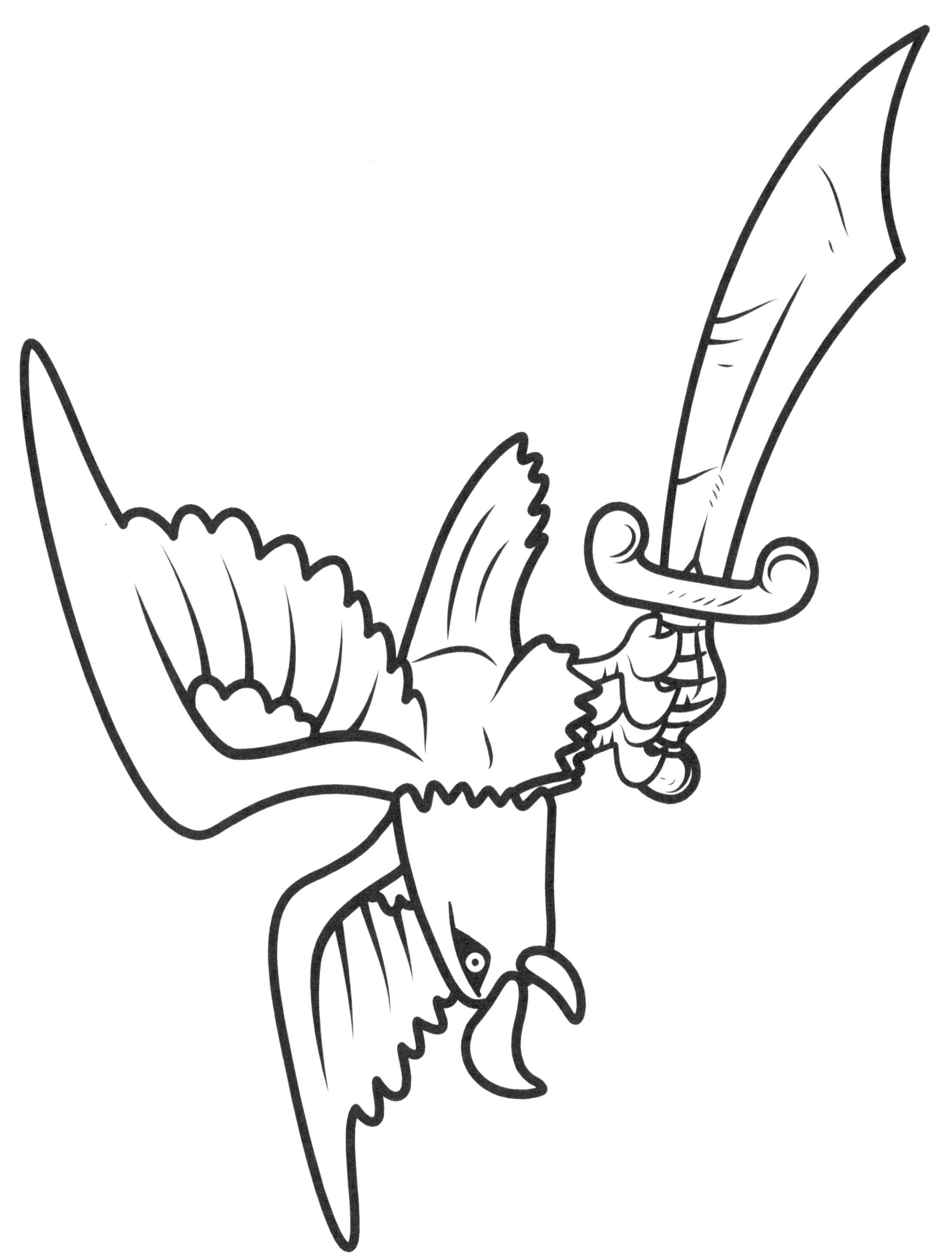

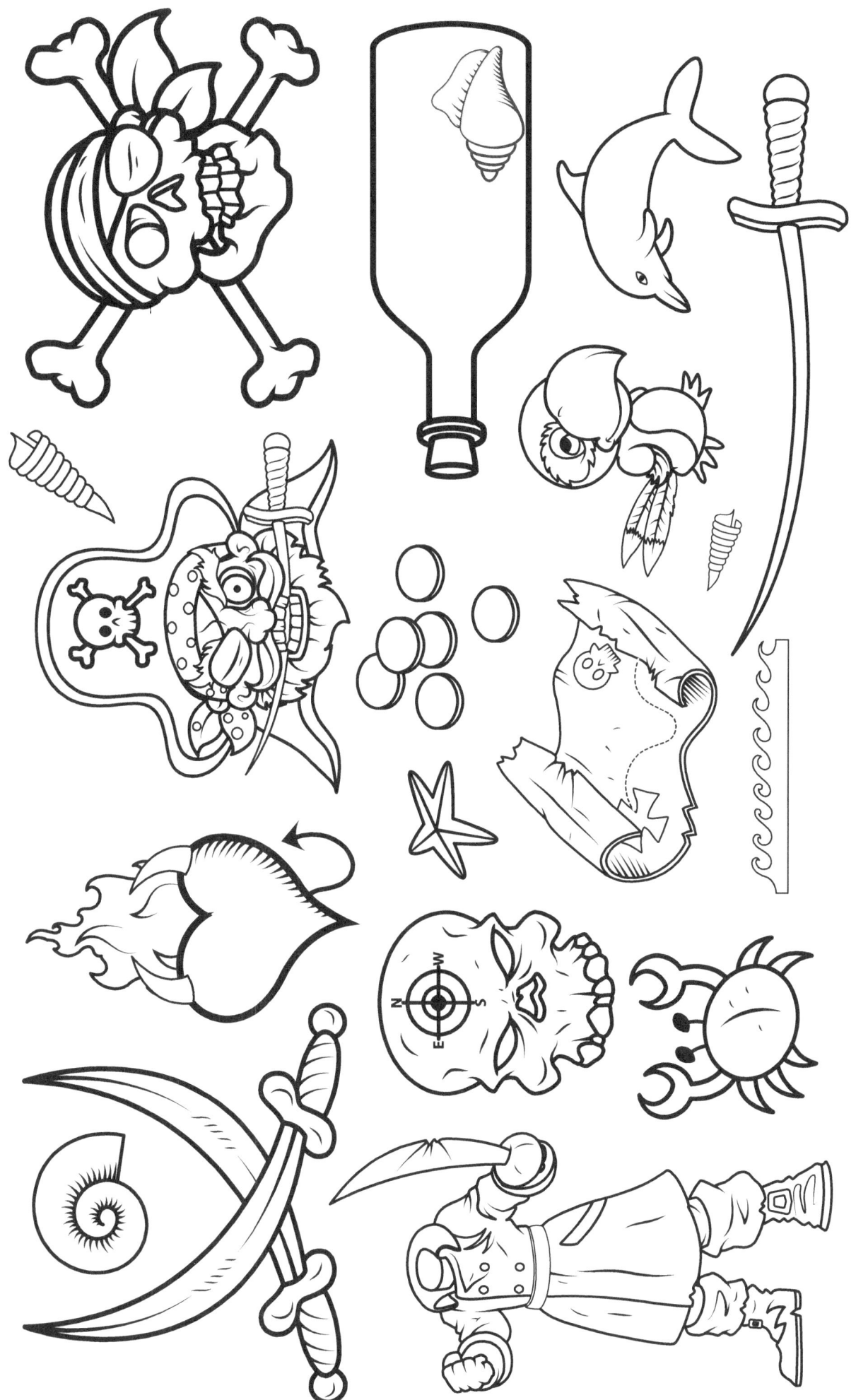

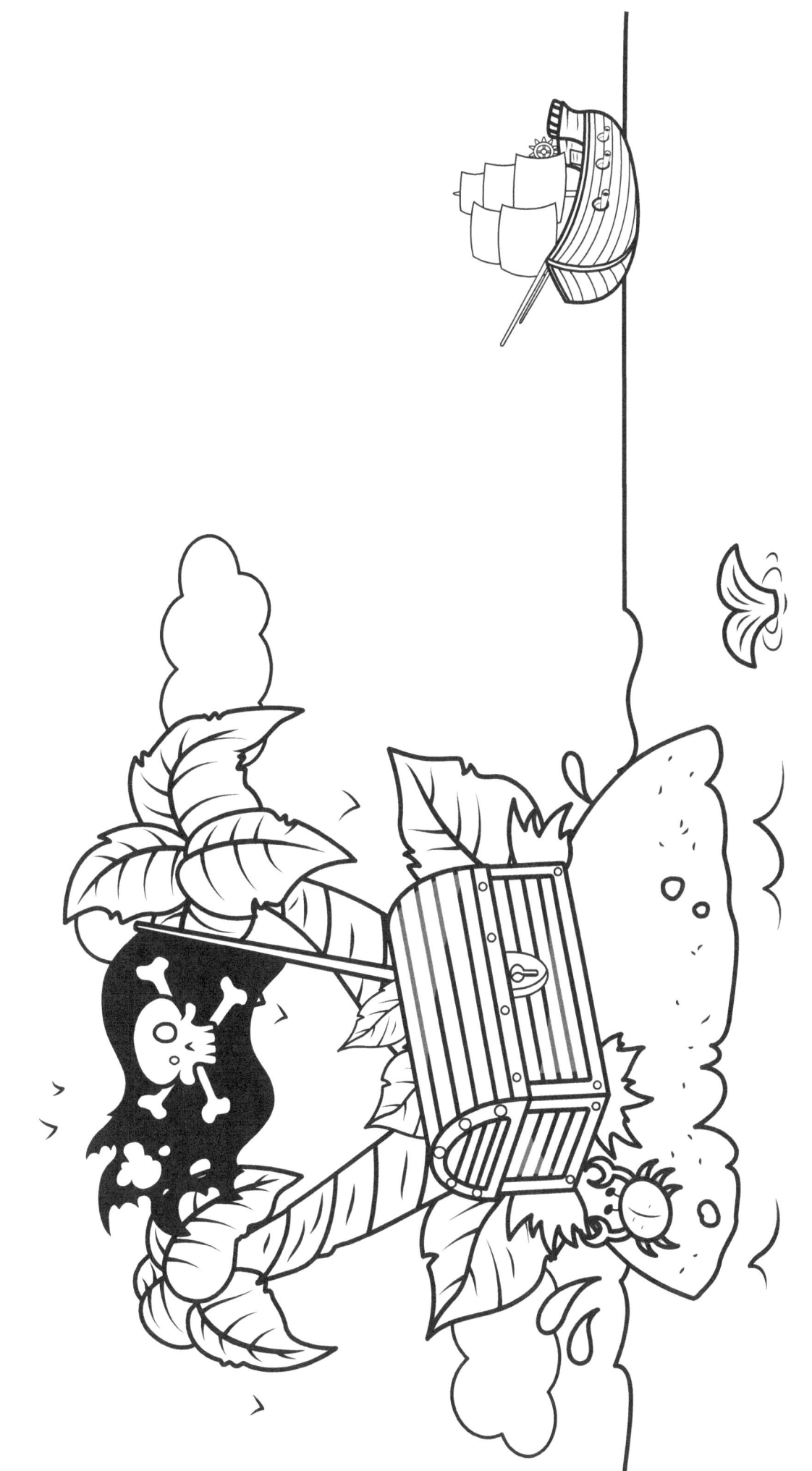

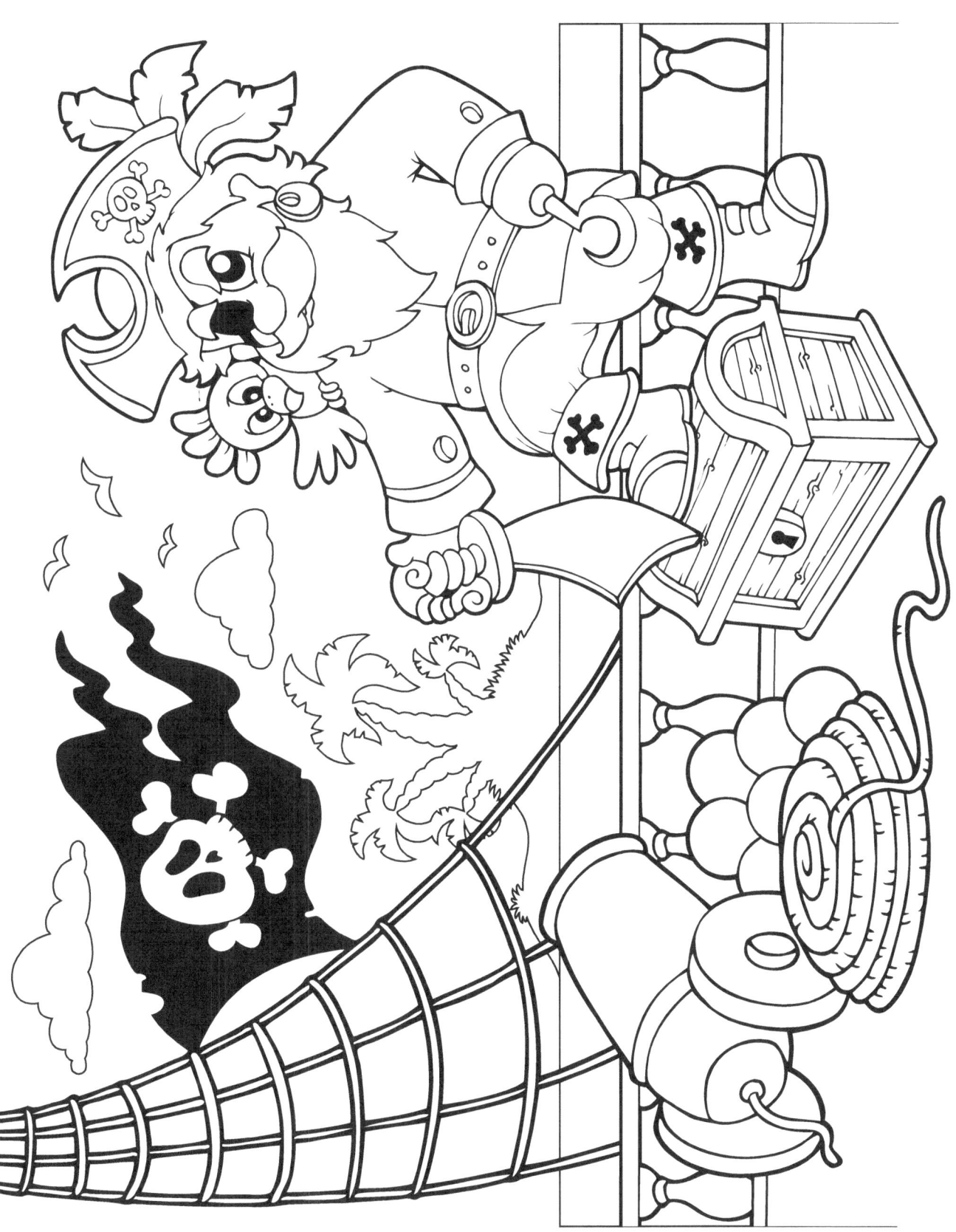

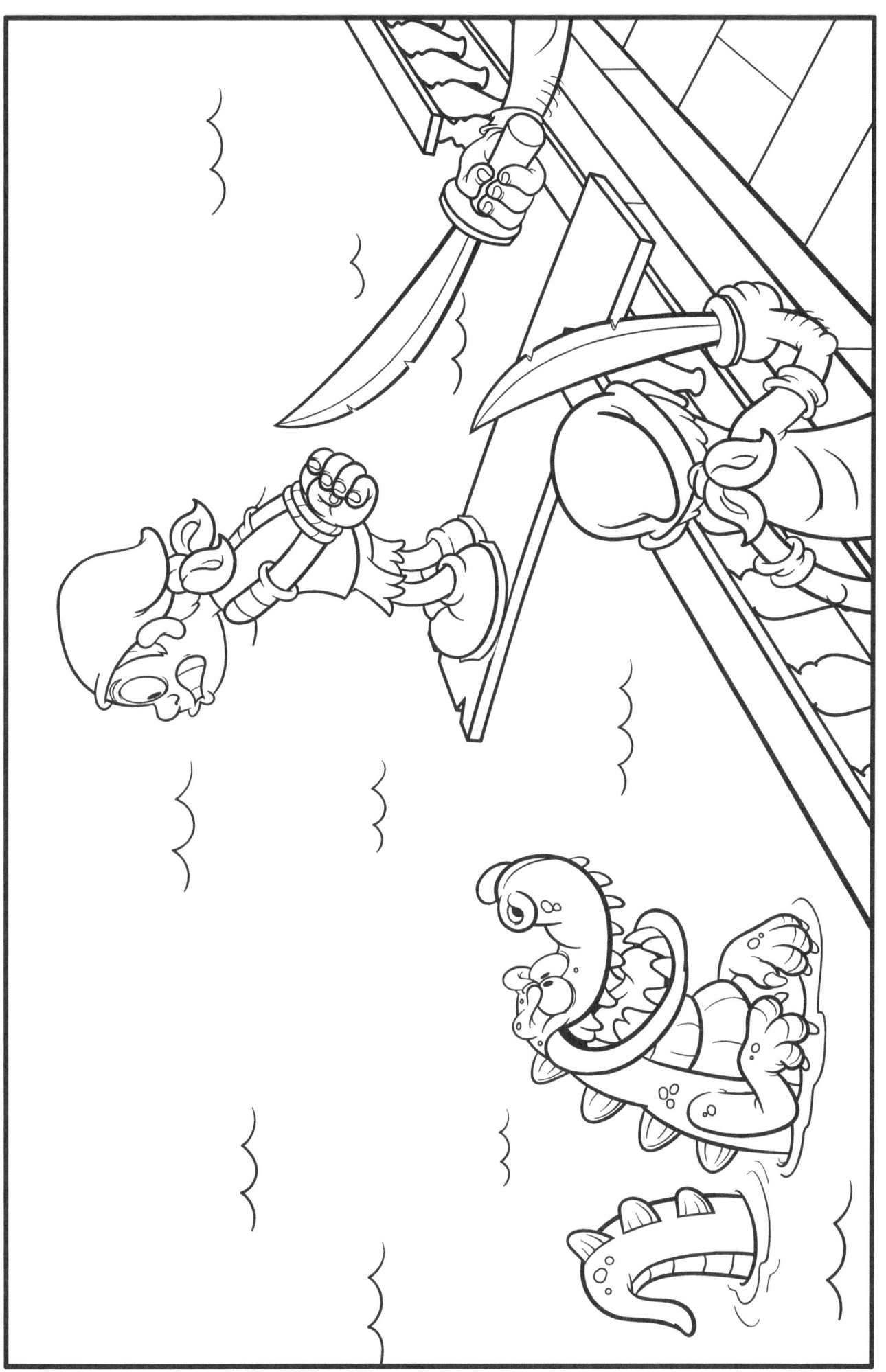

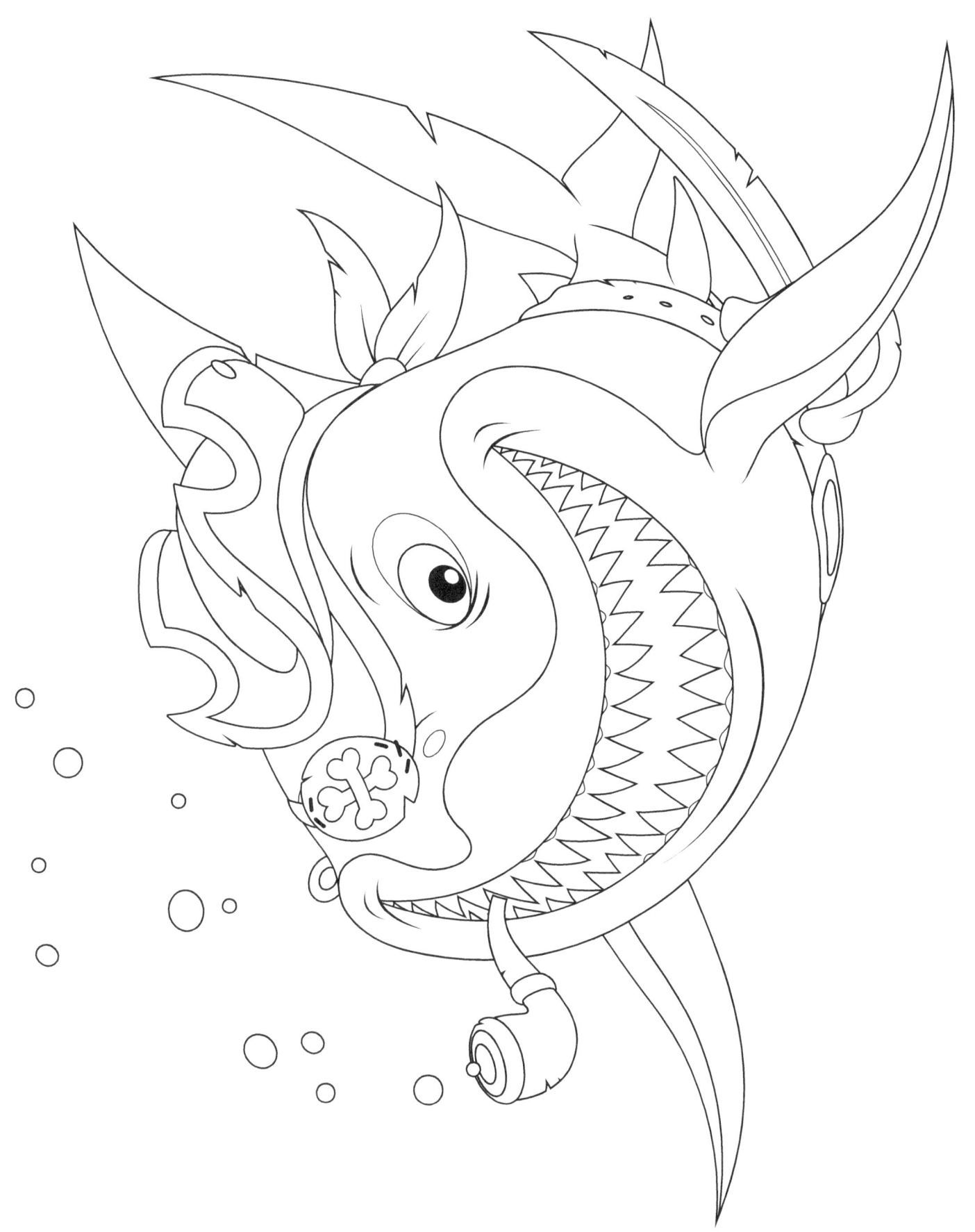

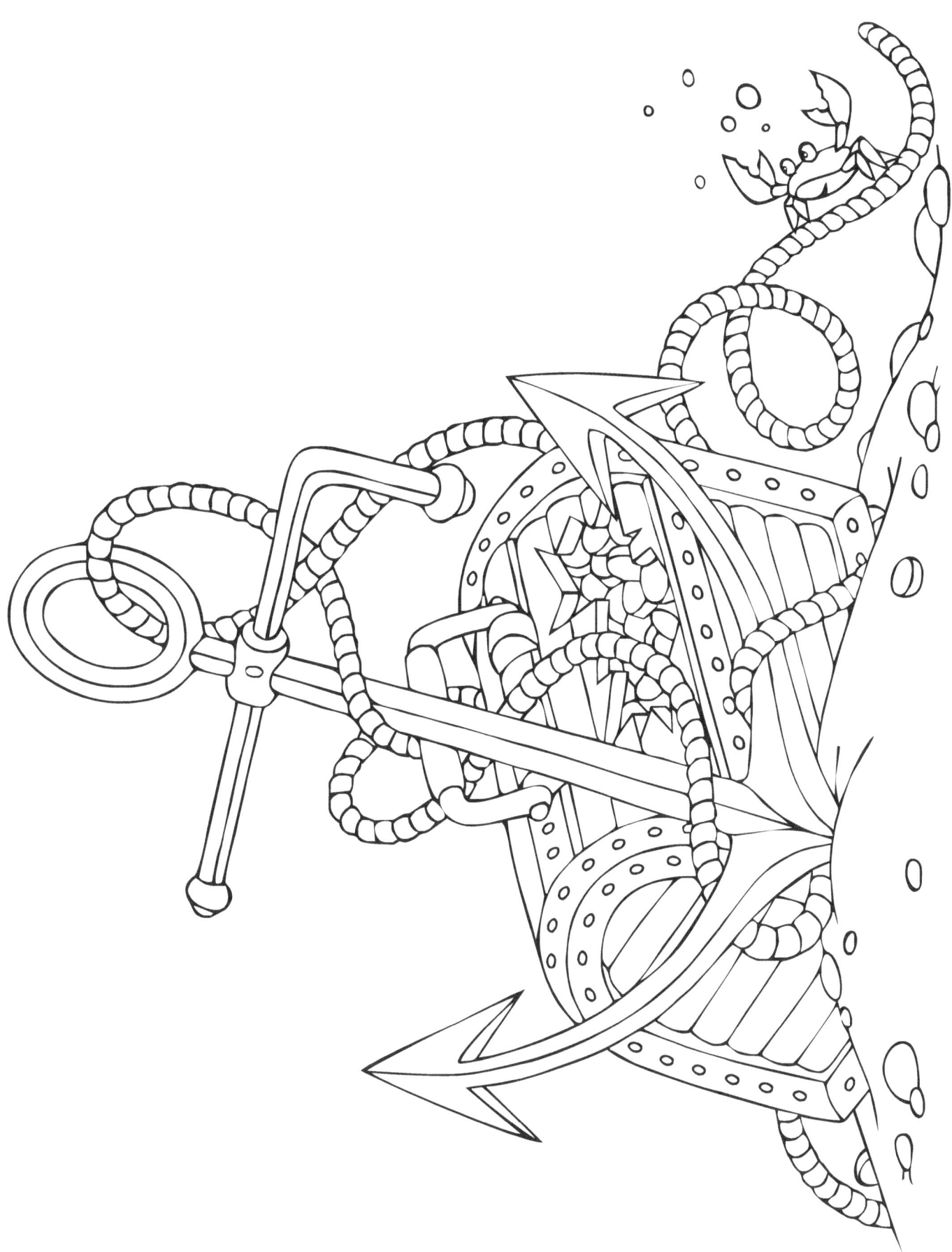

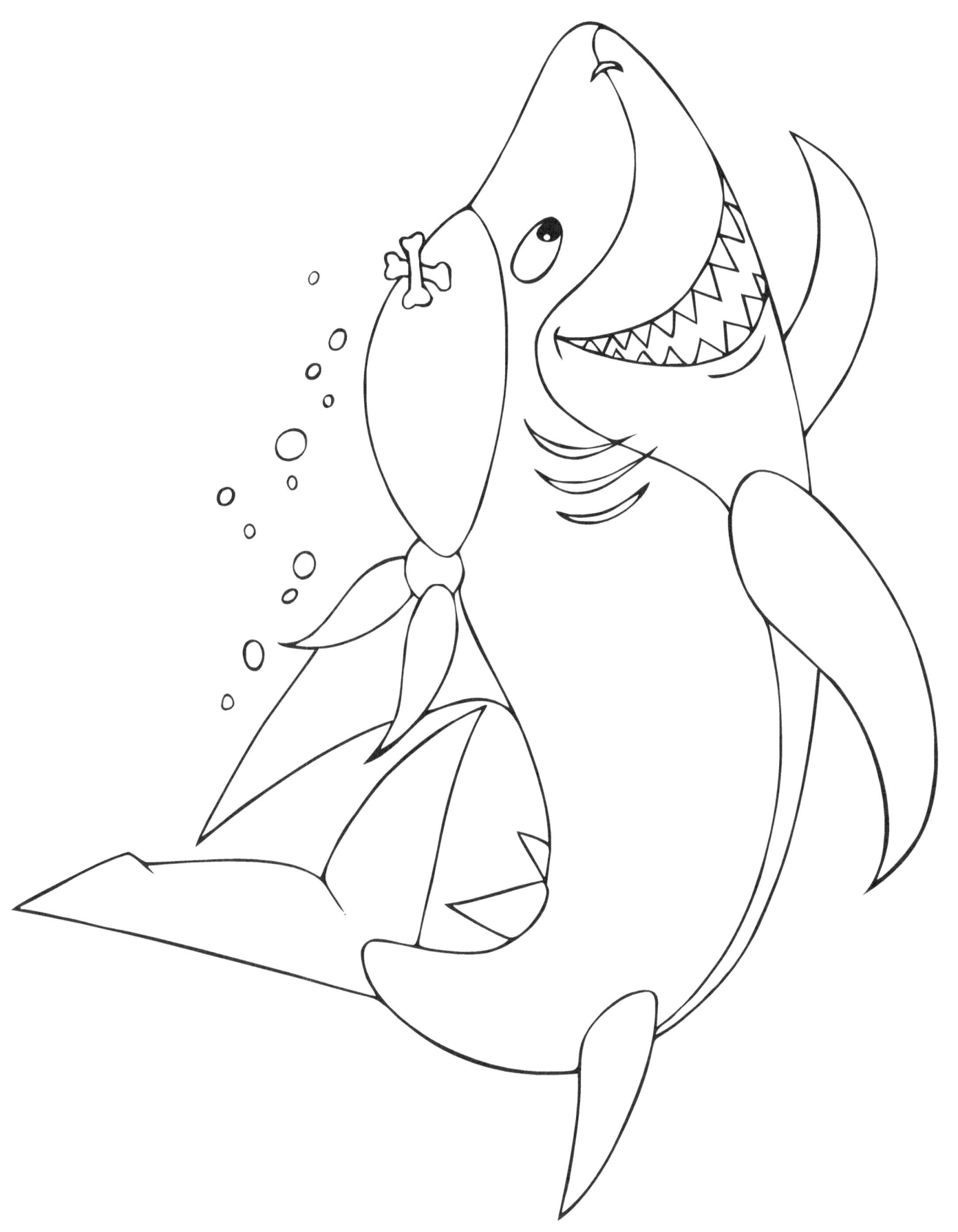

Pirate Coloring Book

Published by:
Art Therapy Coloring
www.arttherapycoloring.com

Images Under License From Shutterstock

www.ingramcontent.com/pod-product-compliance
Lightning Source LLC
Chambersburg PA
CBHW081239180526
45171CB00005B/478